EDUCATION AND THE FAMILY

Papers to mark the
150th Anniversary of
Edmund Rice

Edited by J. Matthew Feheney FPM

VERITAS

First published 1995 by
Veritas Publications
7-8 Lower Abbey Street
Dublin 1

Copyright © J. Matthew Feheney 1995

ISBN 1 85390 305 1

Cover illustration: Icon of Edmund Rice by Desmond Kyne
Printed in the Republic of Ireland by Betaprint Ltd, Dublin

CONTENTS

INTRODUCTION

1994, in addition to being the 150th anniversary of the death of Edmund Rice, a most significant figure in the history of Irish education, was also the UN Year of the Family. It was only to be expected, therefore, that some of the many events organised to mark the 150th anniversary should concentrate on the family. After all, Edmund Rice was a husband and a father before he decided to devote himself to the education of poor boys.

This book began with a conference on Education and the Family at University College, Cork, on 28 May 1994. The conference included both workshops and plenary sessions, the latter including a feature address by Cardinal Cahal B. Daly, a formal response by Dr Frank J. Steele, together with reports, by way of feedback, from the workshops. In the text of his opening address, Cardinal Daly recalls the contribution of Edmund Rice to education, and particularly to Catholic education,. in Ireland. He shows that Edmund was greatly influenced by Nano Nagle, who founded the Presentation Sisters, the first native Irish Congregation since the Reformation. It is for this reason that the Cardinal notes that the entire 'Presentation family', including friends, colleagues and associates, joined together to celebrate the 150th anniversary. Dr Frank J. Steele, in his formal response to the Cardinal's address, recalls the essentials of Edmund Rice's first school and makes this the basis for an outline of what he calls a 'Gospel School'.

Liam Ryan, Aine Hyland, Peter McVerry and Ruth Brennock examine different aspects of the involvement of the family in education: Liam Ryan, as a sociologist, look at the family as system; Aine Hyland, writing from an Irish historical perspective, draws on her specialised knowledge of Irish educational documents; Peter McVerry looks at the influence of the family in preventing or, regrettably sometimes, in promoting juvenile delinquency; Ruth Brennock, President of the National Parents Council (Post-Primary) outlines ways in which parents can help their children to benefit from the educational services offered by schools. She also notes that the children are not the sole beneficiaries of this home-school collaboration: the school and the teachers will also gain considerably.

J. Matthew Feheney tackles the thorny question of the future of Catholic post-primary schools: outlining the challenges to be faced by trustees; recalling the exciting vision of Origen, the first philosopher of the Catholic school, with his challenging aim of engaging in dialogue with other cultures; and emphasising that the school which fosters Gospel values will be more open to Origen's ideal. The same writer joins with Tom O'Keeffe in another article to outline a strategy for exploring the ethos of a Catholic school using a cultural analysis approach.

J.J. Lee examines some of the suggestions in the recent Government Green Paper in the light of the pioneering work and ideals of Edmund Rice. The latter provides a useful touchstone for this evaluation, and the indirect contribution of Edmund and his followers to the early life of the nation, through their past students, is noted. Tony Humphreys writes persuasively on self-esteem: its importance in the intellectual, psychological and emotional growth and development of young people.

Alan McClelland's paper deals with the problems of meeting the educational needs of the Christian family. He presents a theological and philosophical rationale for the Catholic school in the light of the re-affirmation of their importance, not only by Vatican II but, more recently, by Pope John Paul II. This paper, written in the broad context of Catholic education in England, complements that of Brother Feheney, which concentrates on Irish Catholic post-primary schools.

Michael J. Kelleher discusses the painful subjects of suicide and attempted suicide, which, because of their growing frequency, are forcing themselves on our attention. He is especially concerned with the incidence of these problems among young people and the roles of both home and school in combatting these current social problems.

Bernadette Flanagan sensitively examines the issue of Christian feminism, an area with which a significant number of people are still not at ease. In her literature survey, she casts her net wide: trolling not only contemporary feminist writing but also sacred scripture and Papal documents. Not a few will be surprised by the positive statements of Pope John Paul II on the matter.

Not all the papers in this volume were delivered at the conference at UCC in May 1994: the time constraints forced the organisers to defer some papers and workshops but they are included here in the interest of giving a more comprehensive and balanced treatment to the topic. It should also be noted that the conference in Cork was one of four held during the anniversary year: the others, each on a different theme, were held in Belfast, Dublin and Waterford. They were among the hundreds of events held throughout Ireland and England during the anniversary year (1994), a full report of which will be found in the *Edmund Rice 150th Anniversary Yearbook* to be published later this year.

On behalf of the Edmund Rice 150th Anniversary Committee I wish to take this opportunity of thanking UCC for hosting the conference, the contributors of the papers, the distinguished guests, delegates, fáilteoirí and helpers who made the Education Conference on 28 May 1994 in Cork such a memorable event. May they all enjoy reading this book.

J. Matthew Feheney FPM, Editor

EDUCATION AND THE FAMILY: THE LEGACY OF EDMUND RICE

Cardinal Cahal B. Daly

One writer on the history and sociology of religious institutes calculated that the average life expectancy of a religious congregation was one hundred and fifty years. The Brotherhood founded by Edmund Rice has well outlived that span; and, despite dwindling numbers of members in the West, compensated for, however, by increased vocations in Third World countries, it seems certain to survive and flourish far into the future.

Today we are thanking God for Edmund Rice and for the Institute of Brothers which he founded in Waterford in 1802. We are recalling also with thankfulness the links between Edmund Rice and Nano Nagle, and thereby with the Presentation Sisters and the Presentation Brothers. It is, therefore, the Irish Presentation religious family who are joined together in this 150th anniversary celebration. The Brothers and Sisters are joined by Associates, who have pledged themselves to share the Edmund Rice charism and carry it on, with the Brothers, into the future. It is joined also by many lay teachers in the Brothers' schools and by educators from all over Munster.

I say, 'Presentation Family', because Edmund Rice adapted for his Brothers the Rule first drawn up for Nano Nagle's Presentation Sisters. This was itself based on the Rule drawn up for the Visitation Sisters by St Francis de Sales. Brother Rice, in fact, first called his religious society 'The Society of the Presentation of the Blessed Virgin Mary'. The chapters in Nano Nagle's Rule on zeal for the education of the poor, on detachment from worldliness, and on warm community spirit, were those which Edmund particularly cherished, while the devotion to the Blessed Eucharist, the Sacred Heart, and the Passion, inculcated in Nano Nagle's Rule, found an echo in his own heart. At his reception of the habit of religious life, Edmund Rice had taken the religious name of Ignatius. He always regarded Ignatius as a spiritual guide.

The spiritual legacy of Edmund Rice

The foundation of the Institute of Christian Brothers can variously be dated to 1802, when Edmund gathered around him his first small group of young disciples; or to 15 August 1808, when he and his companions first donned the religious habit and pronounced religious vows; or to 1821, when they received Papal approval of their way of prayer and life; or to 1829, when they adopted the new Rule, which was formally published in 1832, after a period of trial.

Before any of these dates, and increasingly since 1802, Edmund had been growing in the interior life and had been eagerly pursuing the *unum necessarium,* the 'one thing necessary'. He avidly read the writings of St Francis de Sales, St Ignatius Loyola, St Teresa of Avila, Alfonso Rodriguez. He cultivated a deep devotion to the Blessed Sacrament and a great love of Our Lady. A decisive influence on Edmund and on his spirituality, Rule and apostolate was, as I have said, that of Nano Nagle. Nano (or Honora) was born nearly fifty years before Edmund. Her Presentation Sisters were the first sisterhood of Irish origin and the Rule drawn up for them was the first such Rule to be drawn up and papally approved for an Irish sisterhood.

It was Nano's personal holiness and her total commitment to the poor which first kindled Edmund's enthusiasm. A Presentation Convent had been provided in Waterford, near Edmund's first monastery of Brothers at Mount Sion; and Edmund observed their life of prayer and poverty and work for the poor with great admiration. It was this admiration which led him to draw upon the Presentation Sisters' Rule in formulating a Rule for his own Brothers.

However, Edmund's life and the beginnings of his Institute were marked by misunderstandings and trials. Some would hold that no religious institute has ever flourished until two conditions are met: first, a row with the bishop of the diocese; second, an internal division and parting of the ways within the community! Some of the Cork Brothers in the North Monastery decided to remain under the direction of the Bishop of Cork as a diocesan institute, while Edmund himself and another group adopted a papal brief approving a new Rule and developed along pontifical lines. The Cork branch became the Presentation Brothers. Both the Presentation Brothers, however, and the Christian Brothers, remained very close in spirituality and in fidelity to Edmund Rice, their common founder, and to his vision of the apostolate. The Presentation Brothers, with the Sisters, are equal sharers in this year's celebrations.

The difference of opinion with the Bishop of Waterford was not unconnected with the question of diocesan status. It is not just out of an instinct to 'close ranks', and 'stand by my own', but in a desire to be objective, that I say that bishops then had to feel that their first priority was the building up of their own diocese after the ravages of the Penal Days. They urgently needed dedicated personnel for the whole range of apostolates or ministries, personnel on whom they could depend for the service of their own people in the fields of spiritual development, religious instruction, education, health, and what we now call social welfare. It was for this reason, and not as part of a greed for power, that they gave preference to diocesan institutes rather than to pontifical institutes, whose members could be assigned anywhere. The resultant tensions were not confined to Ireland, but were found in other countries too, and marked the experience of many religious institutes in their early years. Happily, Edmund's difference of opinion with Bishop Hussey was short-lived and he had excellent relations with Bishop Hussey's successor, Bishop John Power.

Edmund's educational legacy

The achievement of the sons of Edmund Rice in nineteenth- and early twentieth-century Ireland was phenomenal. It has few parallels in any country. The Brothers played a major part in the creation of Catholic education in the desert which was the immediate post-Penal Day Ireland. They provided free education for the poor long before the term was even coined at a time when the State was totally opposed to Catholic education as such and when its contribution to education was minimal. Many of the men who created the Irish State, many of the men who formed its early governments, who staffed its civil service, who played leading roles in the cultural, educational and social development of the country, were 'Christian Brothers' boys' or 'Presentation Brothers' boys'. Their past pupils are still as numerous and as distinguished. The work of the Presentation Sisters is no less outstanding.

The Christian Brothers are sometimes accused of having inculcated an extreme and narrow nationalism. I believe that the charge is exaggerated. It must be remembered that the Irish people in the nineteenth and early twentieth centuries needed a sense of identity, a feeling of pride and confidence in being Irish, a spirit of independence. They needed what we might now call 'empowerment'. Nationalism can be taken for granted when it has been accorded its place among the nations of the earth; it may need more emphatic expression when it has not yet won freedom, equality and independence. Ireland owes an immense debt to the Brothers for helping its people, empowering its people, to believe in themselves, to take pride in their own language and culture and history. If some feel superior to the Brothers' early educational programmes today, it may be because they are standing on the Brother's shoulders when they think that they are standing on the moral higher ground.

Edmund's spiritual legacy

Edmund Rice had a passionate predeliction for the poor. Nevertheless, his primary motivation was his passionate love for God. He did not set out to organise a group of dedicated teachers, but to form a group of men in love with God and to prepare them for a life lived for God's glory. He sought first the Kingdom of God, and this is why so much was added on to him in terms of temporal achievement.

In the Christian Brothers' Rule of 1882 we find the following:

> The Spirit of this Institute is that spirit of faith, to do nothing but with a view to God and to ascribe all to God. ... thus they will preserve the spirit of disengagement from creatures. Each one on entering it is to leave father, mother, etcetera, and all he possesses in the world; ... to live only for Christ; ...and to accept and desire with all possible eagerness what Christ loved and embraced in order to

resemble Jesus Christ, who has given us the example and who is the way, and the truth and the life that leads to glory. ...Finally, the Spirit of the Institute is an ardent zeal for the instruction of children, for rearing them up in the fear and love of God.

Edmund lived this life himself first, and then by example and a kind of spiritual contagion led many others to live it too. By his heavenly intercession he has helped, and continues to help, many thousands of Brothers to live this life as he lived it. If vocations have declined, perhaps this may be in some part because we have developed a too horizontalist understanding of Christian life, perhaps even of religious life. All religious are invited, particularly in the wake of Vatican II, to return to the sources, to rediscover the Founder's or Foundress's charism; and this return, this rediscovery, will always reveal that the first concern of the Founder or Foundress was the sanctification of the Brothers or Sisters, through the following of Jesus Christ and the living of the Gospel by way of the evangelical counsels. The apostolate of the great Founders and Foundresses flowed from contemplation. 'God first served' was their priority.

Edmund Rice would have stressed that the primary ministry of Brothers in the Church is not any particular apostolic activity or pastoral service, even the education or service of the poor. Rather, it is a ministry of holiness and prayer. The first and most important contribution which Brothers can make to the work of the Church is to radiate her holiness by the holiness of their own lives, to make the Kingdom of God present in the world through their own total dedication to the Kingdom. It is not primarily by what they do but by what they are that consecrated men and women serve the Church and transform the world.

I fear that, in our understandable and necessary zeal to promote vocations, we have sometimes laid the primary stress on the invaluable services which religious congregations offer to society, in such fields as education, health care, welfare, charitable organisations and activities, etc. We have taken legitimate pride in the record of our religious institutes in the fields of service. We have presented religious life as a challenging and relevant way of helping our fellow men and women. All this is certainly true. And yet it misses the essential point. I believe that relatively few, even in the past when vocations were plentiful, entered religious life primarily for the sake of helping their fellow men and women or of rendering a specific professional service. Fewer still of those for whom this was the primary motivation have remained in religious life.

It is my conviction that people should not be invited to enter religious life today primarily for motives of service of others. I believe that there is, in the last analysis, no adequate reason for becoming a religious except that of desiring to give one's whole life to God, seeking closer union with Jesus Christ, pursuing holiness, taking the Gospel literally and desiring to live totally the call of Christ: 'Come, follow me'. It is one index of an increasingly secular society that it is rarely any longer seen to be self-evident that the necessary and sufficient motive for entering religious life is that one desires to 'be forever with the Lord'. A God-oriented society regards it as self-evidently a privilege to be called to such a life. A man-centred and this-world-centred society looks for motivation and for value solely in the service of human beings. The Christian sees the two as being inseparably connected; but gives unhesitating primacy to the love and worship and service of God.

Edcation and the family

I am conscious that I have not yet addressed the main theme of this Conference, 'Education and the Family'. The theme is well chosen, for this is the International Year of the Family. Pope John Paul has again and again declared that the family is at the heart of the life of the Church and at the heart of the life of society. He called a special Synod of Bishops in 1980 to reflect on the importance of the family. In his final document, presenting the conclusions of the Synod, the Holy Father declared:

> The future of the world and of the Church passes through the family. The future of humanity passes by way of the family.
>
> (*Familiaris consortio*)

Rarely has the family had greater problems to face than it has at the present day. Attempts are being made in some quarters to change the very meaning of the family and to introduce new legal definitions of family which would no longer require marriage, no longer imply the presence in a child's life of a father and mother, or even presuppose for a baby's conception any personal relationship whatever between its two parents. Distinctions are being made between 'biological parents' and 'birth parents', between 'surrogate parents' and 'natural parents'. We all need to reflect again on the grace and vocation of the Catholic family. We need to protect the place which properly belongs to the family in the life and in the laws of society. We need to recognise the primordial place of the family in education and we must try to give real meaning in education to the traditional phrase which says that teachers act *in loco parentis*. When parents are busy or negligent or violent, we must do our best to supply the missing dimension of love in their lives. Children need love as much as they need food. A child deprived of love is stunted in its personal growth. In a very striking phrase Pope John Paul says that children deprived of love are 'morally orphans'.

Religion in the home
Edmund Rice's greatest distress today would have been the spiritual deprivation which exists in so many families. The first lesson he would have wanted to teach would have been the lesson about how God loves each child and how special and precious each child is to Him. The worst of all forms of child neglect is neglect of their formation in the knowledge of God and his love, and in faith and prayer. Shockingly, a few children, because of what they hear at home and in the street, seem to think that the name 'Jesus' is a swear word rather than the holy name. Roddy Doyle's *The Family* is a frightening illustration of the challenge confronting us in some places and among some sectors of Irish society.

While schools and teachers cannot be expected to solve the problems of society, or to undo the harm which society itself does to children, it remains true that the Catholic school cannot fulfil its mission in isolation from the home, the parish and the community. We must do all that we can to encourage collaboration between school, home and parish, between teacher, parent, priests and parish pastoral team. The Synod on Catechetics, in an unexpected phrase, declared the parish to be the primary locus of catechetics. It is the parish community which has the responsibility of handing on the faith. The school is its greatest means for discharging this duty; the commitment and generosity of parishioners and parents in providing the voluntary contribution required to establish and to maintain Catholic schools is an indication of the community's willingness to accept this responsibility. But setting up a school does not absolve the community of any further responsibility. They must continue to support the work of the school and to support the teachers in their task.

Especially, they must support the religious education programmes in the school, taking an interest in the children's religion lessons, their workbooks and projects, their prayers. The home should be a domestic church; it should also be a partner with the school in the task of Christian formation of the young.

Many programmes are available nowadays to help us to move towards this ideal. We have parenting programmes, the *Growing in Faith Together* programme; we have *Search* and many other programmes for young people. The involvement of teachers in these programmes is immensely helpful. I am full of admiration for the willingness of so many teachers, well beyond any line of professional duty, to assist with such programmes and to involve themselves in their operation. Home-school-community liaison needs to be developed. The parish must be conscientised about its responsibility in these areas.

The great instrument of Christian conscientisation is the small ecclesial community, deeply formed in faith, imbued with love of God and of the Church, filled with enthusiasm for the Gospel, radiating the Good News of Jesus Christ. These groups can be leaven in the loaf for the wider parish and for society as a whole. The faith animation of small groups is, I believe, one of the signs of the times in today's Church, one of the major ways forward for the Church in our time. The brotherhoods and the sisterhoods will not be found wanting in this challenge and in forming their lay teachers and parents in planning these new approaches to evangelisation. All of these endeavours would certainly meet with full and enthusiastic commendation from Edmund Ignatius Rice.

Brotherhoods face the future

As I turn in conclusion to look at the future of the Christian and Presentation Brothers and of religious brotherhoods in general, I feel that one could find no better words than those spoken by Pope John Paul to brothers in Maynooth in 1979:

> I wish to speak a special word to religious brothers. The past decade has brought great changes, and with them problems and trials unprecedented in all your previous experience. I ask you not to be discouraged. Be men of great truth, of great and unbounded hope. ... The past decade has also brought a great renewal of your understanding of your holy vocation, a great deepening of your liturgical lives and your prayer, a great extension of the field of your apostolic influence. I ask God to bless you with renewed fidelity in vocation among your members and with increased vocations to your institutes. The Church in Ireland and on the missions owes much to all the Institutes of Brothers. Your call to holiness is a precious adornment of the Church. Believe in your vocation. Be faithful to it. 'God has called you and He will not fail you'. (1 Thess 5:23)

A community of brothers who live by faith, who 'try to grow perfect, help one another, be united and live in peace' (2 Cor 13:11) in real and realistic community love, who cherish the freedom with which Christ makes them free in chastity and poverty and obedience, who rejoice with the joy of the Good News and look forward in joyful hope in expectation of the Lord's coming, such a community provides a compelling witness to the world of the reality of the personal and living Christ. The life of such a community might be called, in the words of Joachim Jeremias, a series of signs and examples of 'the sort of thing that happens when the Kingdom breaks through'.

That, I believe, is the essence both of the life of the religious and of his witness in the world. The life of the religious brother is, above all else, a life of faith in the Gospel and a witness to the world of the truth and relevance and power of the Gospel. Religious will always be the men and women who can say with Saint Paul: 'I am not ashamed of the Gospel: It is the power of God saving all who have faith'. (Romans 1:16).

> So, in the words of the writer of the Letter to the Hebrews: Hold up your limp arms and steady your trembling knees… then the injured limb will not be wrenched, it will grow strong again… Since the things being shaken are created things, they are going to be changed so that the unshakeable things will be left. We have been given possession of an unshakeable kingdom. Let us therefore hold on to the grace that we have been given…. For our God is a consuming fire. (Heb 12:13. 27-29).

My final prayer for you, my dear Brothers, and my confident hope, is expressed in the words of Saint Paul, which were quoted for you by Pope John Paul in Maynooth:

> May the God of hope bring you such joy and peace in your faith that the power of the Holy Spirit will remove all bounds to hope. (Romans 15:13).

PARENTS, CHURCH AND SCHOOL: MEETING THE EDUCATIONAL NEEDS OF THE CHRISTIAN FAMILY

V.A. McClelland

Writing some fifteen years ago, Philip Coombs, founding director of UNESCO's International Institute for Educational Planning, startled many contemporary theorists by identifying religious and moral education rather than the growth of technological and science education as the fundamental challenge confronting education in the twenty-first century. In *The World Crisis in Education,* Coombs wrote:

> The debate over the issue will remain lively and important throughout the world as long as cultural upheavals continue, and as long as the morality taught by the schools and by the great religions (and preached, if not always practised, by politicians) continues to clash with 'the morality embodied and embedded in modern industry, commerce and finance'. The issue will be resolved in different ways in different societies or left unresolved. But no society can remain indifferent to it. Nor is indifference possible for anyone involved in education, from top policy makers to classroom teachers. Sooner or later each must think the issue through, decide where he or she really stands on the matter, and act accordingly.'[1]

Twenty years before Coombs wrote this, Vatican II was saying much the same thing in its specific Declaration on Christian Education (*Gravissimum educationis*). While located within the wider context of *Lumen gentium* and *Gaudium et spes,* the document on Christian education was concerned to restate the age-old tradition of the Church on schools and schooling and to delineate a number of major principles which continued to inspire it in effecting Christ's command to teach all nations.

Fundamentally, the Council states the inalienable right of all men and women to education, a right not to be thwarted by issues of race, age, sex or social conditions. True education is directed towards *the formation of the human person* in view of our final end and the good of our fellow human beings. Secondly, we are told, this inalienable right to education carries with it *the right to a Christian education,* characterised by an unfolding exposé of the mystery of salvation and a growth in appreciation of the gift of faith. The third principle enunciated emphasised *the rights and duties of parents* in the educative process, stressing their obligation to provide *an integrated, personal and social education* for their children. Other agencies have important participatory roles in this process, not least society itself and its representative governments, but, above all, *the Church,* in her duty 'of proclaiming the way of salvation to all men, of revealing the life of Christ to those who believe, and of assisting them with unremitting care so that they may be able to attain to the fullness of that life.'[2]

This later statement leads naturally to a consideration of the importance of catechetical instruction, 'which illumines and strengthens the faith' and 'stimulates a conscious and fervent participation in the liturgical mystery' and the active apostolate. The logical progression is then to consider the importance of the Catholic school which has the dual function of 'nurturing the intellectual faculties' in common with all schools and introducing pupils to the cultural (for which read 'religious') heritage bequeathed to them. In this way the Catholic school fosters a sense of right values and prepares its children for the world of work against a background of faith and mutual understanding. Parents, because of their fundamental responsibility for the education of their children, should have full freedom, in partnership with the State, to select a Christian school which will help them to fulfil their duty. *Gravissimum educationis* emphasises also the Church's obligation to its children who are not educated, for a variety of reasons, in a Catholic school. They too should be provided with teaching in Christian Doctrine, reinforcing the religious and cultural inheritance of the family.

The document then introduces the word *community.* A Catholic education has a special role in forging and developing a spirit of community in 'an atmosphere animated by a spirit of liberty and charity based on the Gospel'. This concept of community 'orients the whole of human culture to the message of salvation' in such a way that 'the knowledge which the pupils acquire of the world of life and of men is illumined by faith.'[3] The Catholic school in pursuit of such a goal envisages the formation of its children so that they may become a 'saving leaven' in the wider societal community of which they are also a part. In this matter of the forging of a community, teachers are warned that 'it depends chiefly on them whether the Catholic school achieves its purpose'.

More specific issues concerning the concept of Catholic education are left to the post-conciliar pronouncements to develop, especially the *General Catechetical Directory* of 1971, the statement entitled *Catholic Schools* issued by the Sacred Congregation for Catholic Education in 1977, the document *Lay Catholics in Schools, Witnesses to Faith* issued by the same Congregation in 1982, and its important pronouncement on *The Religious Dimension of Education in a Catholic School,* published in 1988, in which it is argued that the Catholic school must be more than an educational centre: it must be a place of authentic apostolate and pastoral action, reaching out into the wider community and adding essential Christian witness to the cultivation of traditional civic virtues. The Catholic school is thus seen to be involved in missionary enterprise, perhaps even the missionary arm of the Church. It is in this approach that we see the essence of change in the Church's attitude to the witness of the Catholic school. It was a change anticipated in England by the late Archbishop George Andrew Beck, then Bishop of Salford, when he wrote in 1963 that the Catholic involvement in education ought not to be to support a sort of ghetto subculture but to ensure that the full richness of faith was brought to bear upon the secularised and desacritised world it had perforce to encounter.[4]

Throughout the conciliar and post-conciliar documents on education, certain words and phrases appear and reappear which in themselves underscore the concept of Catholic education as it has been understood since Pius XI's attempt to systematise it in 1929 in *Divini illius magistri* – terms such as *formation of the human person, nurture, wholeness, integration* and *community.*

Underlying the use of such terms is the Church's commitment to *family*, in the widest context of that concept.

To be a Catholic, one writer has recently told us, means to be 'bonded with millions of other people not only throughout the world, but also through time. Those who have gone on before us in faith are still living members of the body of Christ and in some unimaginable way we are all connected.'[5] We use the term 'communion of saints' to embrace this theological concept, this idea of organic connection with the whole human family of God's creation *in Christo*. Vatican II has taught us to keep this view of the human family before us when we think of the Catholic school and Catholic education. Within that concept, ecclesial tradition, moral realism, Christian hope and spiritual fulfilment achieve meaningful relationship. Only within that wider framework, as Kenneth Woodward has recently pointed out, can family life, influenced as it is by biological, psychological, social and emotional ties, be seen to be of spiritual worth and significance. When the Church uses the term 'family', then, it has before it the fact that we are all part of the communion of saints. Preparation for 'the good life', therefore, must not lose sight of the tradition of the Church in its exposition of Catholic doctrine and Christian moral teaching. It is still too little understood, and indeed, considered to be perhaps too revolutionary a view – in our society, as Woodward puts it, 'to assert that all human beings are radically connected over space, through time and even beyond death'. Such a view 'is to counter the experience and assumptions of western, free-enterprising societies which prize personal autonomy and the individual self. In such societies, even the observable connective tissue that once held people together – of marriage, (human) family, (human) community, of blood, soil and social purpose, are experienced as arbitrary limitations on the primacy and sovereignty of the self.'[6]

The Church's insistence on the provision of Catholic schools that have the communion of saints at the very heart of their concept of family, community, wholeness and integration presents a serious challenge to a society whose entire world is delimited by space, time and material objectives and whose educational philosophy is all too often circumscribed by the individualistic, utilitarian and self-expressive mores of secular beings. This is the nub of the Church's insistence on the necessity for Catholic schools: its schools are thus seen not simply as places where Catholic children are to be immersed in what is often termed a Catholic ethos, surrounded by religious observances and the proverbial smell of incense, in the hope that they will miraculously grow up with a knowledge of the beliefs and practices of their faith that will somehow provide a sound spiritual bedrock for the remainder of their lives. The concepts of witness, challenge and example are not to be lost sight of. Catholic children are not simply *to cope* with the world while preserving their own spiritual integrity, they are to challenge it and change it, by prayer surely, but also by the quality of their own lives, the strengths of their beliefs, their wholeness within the communion of saints, and their faith in action.

In *Understanding Christian Nurture,* a document issued by the British Council of Churches a decade ago, we see the issue from a non-Catholic religious stance. 'Christian nurture', it declared, 'can appear to be rather parochial, rather narrow, offering only constricted horizons to young people, while secular education presents itself as open, all-embracing, allied with scientific discovery, able, through a multitude of techniques and aids, to offer the widest opportunities to all.' It fearfully posed the question, would not, under such circumstances, Christian nurture 'seem to be concerned with its own survival rather than with the genuine wellbeing of the young'?[7] Such a timorous caveat cannot be levied at a Christian education which places the communion of saints as its *raison d'être.* Instead of being concerned with the goal of human independence as if it were the only desirable objective, it is motivated by Christian interdependence, impelled by a just sense of Christian teaching, a love for others and for God's creation, and a hope transcending the grave and the cruelties and misfortunes of life. In such a commitment, freely entered into and accepted, a robust witness to the heritage of Christianity is presented. *Understanding Christian Nurture* has itself pointed out that there can be no value in merely being an alternative to a secular State school system *per se.* Denominational schools must, in their teaching and their structures, explicitly and implicitly allow the light of the Christian Gospel to search the value assumptions of contemporary life and education.[8]

In Catholic schools we need material reminders, too, of this transcendence: the crucifix should not be discarded from the classroom as a gesture to religious pluralism, neither should the representation of saints be relegated to the dust cupboards in the interests of false ecumenism. Nor should pious religious habits be abandoned on the specious claim of avoiding indoctrinatory practices. All these things are daily reminders of the communion of saints which lies at the heart of the theology of the Catholic school. Such schools will not overcome the materialism of the age by assiduously accommodating themselves to its outward manifestations. It may seem a trivial point to some, but the richness or otherwise of the Christian environment of a school has much to communicate about the mission statement of that school.

William Kopp used to assert that children '*catch* an enthusiasm' and '*respond* to an ideal' and, with him, we accept the corollary that 'wholeness' is not a term we reserve for adulthood – 'a child is a whole person regardless of his age.'[9] The reception of the sacrament of baptism enables a child to share fully in the fellowship of the community life. As a consequence, as Colin Aloes has written, the child must be enabled to feel 'a sense of belonging which is just as deep as the adult's'.[10] Thus he will absorb the 'shared beliefs, values and attitudes' which permeate the school community as a whole. Nurturing of this kind will have a goal of autonomy of belief as the ambience of the child's adult life. Catholics ought not to be ashamed, thus, of the admission that the intent and purpose of their denominational schools is a missionary intent. Perhaps it was because sight had been lost of this design that it was necessary to issue the General Catechetical Directory of 1971 and every hierarchy was urged to formulate its own national directory.

Unity of purpose and order in practice are not yet characteristic of all Catholic schools and in England and Wales, for instance, as reliance on religious education schemes such as *Weaving the Web* has come to predominate, Catholicism seems to be less of a distinguishing feature than it was hitherto. Michael Lee has described a similar situation in parts of the United States, which he finds disquieting 'when it is recalled that the primary reason why parents send their children to Catholic schools is to deepen and enhance their offspring's religious understanding and life style.'[11] Perhaps a corrective to this weakness is to take to heart some of the verbal lessons propounded by the present Conservative administration in England and involve priests, parents, children, teachers and the parish community in identifying the Catholic teaching they expect the children to receive in a Catholic school. Here would be a real spirit of community endeavour which would obviate the necessity of leaving the planning to so-called catechetical pundits who have not been spectacularly successful in the schemes they have advanced.

Bishop Patrick Kelly of Salford outlined the importance of the synthesis under discussion here in giving his reasons why the existence of Catholic schools should be defended. In *Catholic Schools* (1987), he wrote:

> We are convinced that our discipleship is not something which is alongside the rest of life: it is the beginning, the context and the goal of all our living. We therefore do not see the various elements which are part of a young person's formation as fragmented and unrelated. They must all find their place, nourish and be nourished by the Word of God revealed to us in our Lord. For us it would be false to the whole truth to say that subjects can be taught in some neutral fashion with formal religious education offered alongside them. For us neutral education is a loss of the wholeness offered to us in Our Lord. And therefore our service to the whole educational enterprise is not accomplished by becoming part of a 'series ... ' system where the various elements are offered in isolation from an overall vision. Our contribution must be education seen as a wholesome endeavour, related to a community's vision and way of life. A Catholic school requires a shared vision which is clearly perceived, articulated and presented as its life and reason for existence. Our service of all schooling is the testimony of schools rooted in a community with a shared vision and whose schooling is therefore integrated and wholesome.[12]

We notice in this quotation the key words being used once again – shared vision, formation, nourishment, wholeness, integration and community – a traditional and orthodox view. But does it represent reality?

If we are to revitalise our approach to Catholic education by bringing about a realisation of the importance of individual worth to the process of making society more conscious of the things of the Spirit, to the constructing of a society which has Christocentric attitudes towards those in need as well as towards the right use of possessions, wealth and power, it is important that the Catholic school be a microcosm of a community in which Christian values are clearly in operation.

It is here that we find some Catholic schools do not convey conviction. Mary Warnock, in her telling little book *Schools of Thought,* has written cogently on this particular problem of the divide between theory and practice, pointing out that patterns of behaviour emerge from real contexts, not merely from exemplary ones: 'a man does not have to prove to us that he has acted well. We can learn that he has, from experience'.[13]

If we are to create the kind of 'ethos' in our Catholic schools which meets Bishop Kelly's objective – an objective, incidentally, identified by Don Bosco in the nineteenth century as really the interplay of reason, religion and love (interpreted in practice as loving-kindness, charity to others and concern for all)[14] then much greater study and planning in respect of identifying that ethos needs to be undertaken and consideration given as to how it can be generated and sustained. One thing is certain, that it does not arise or proceed effectively in a haphazard fashion as at times we seem content to hope.

An ethos is *created* and it implies identification of shared vision, ideals and the structuring of a sympathetic environment in which it can flourish. Above all, perhaps, are needed teachers of vision to develop it. There has to be a recognition and an agreement that the Catholic ethos is central to all the work of the school, that it is pervasive throughout the school, that it has a measure of perceived stability, that it constitutes the unifying element in the curriculum and that it is accepted by parents and the Catholic community upon whose support the school relies. All this represents a corpus of hard work and devotion to duty on the part of all members of the school and parochial community, and cannot be taken for granted. The key to its success can be found in Dudley Plunkett's view that 'far more than any trade or profession, Christianity is met experientially and continuously as a vocation in community, shared responsibility, and identification with the other, the neighbour, and with Christ.'[15] Christianity, he reminds us, 'is about constantly transcending the idols we all have, to overcome fragmentation, conflict, sectarianism, ideologies, and all kinds of divisions' in our lives.[16]

The holistic nature of the Catholic ideal, therefore, must 'define a kind of school and schooling that would exemplify caring, community, reconciliation, forgiveness, prayer and witness, just as these define the kind of society as a whole that Christians should be seeking.'[17] It follows, therefore, that the Catholic school must aim at being a microcosm of the Christian society we all desiderate. Self-fulfilment is not neglected. After all, the latter is not something overtly sought: it is a by-product, as the late Professor M.V.C. Jeffreys never tired of saying, 'of the life in which the self is lost in something more than self.' Self-fulfilment can be found in that form of Christian endeavour which gives without measuring the cost.

Of course, if a Catholic school is to retain its credibility with parents and the secular world, it has to show an equal concern with what the world understands by the making of persons – the preparation to earn a livelihood, the need to develop particular aptitudes, skills and gifts, the desire to provide for centres of human interest and gratification. In England, the Catholic school needed no other stimulus to be conscious of this challenge than that provided by the Thatcherite democracy of the 1980s and 90s and its legislative enactment of 1988 with the prescription for a national curriculum based upon the philosophy that work, achievement, productivity and monetary reward are the real corner-stones of democratic education in a free society; with its disingenuous appeals to parental choice and the need for open enrolment influenced by a sharp competitiveness resting upon published league tables of examination successes; and, even more significantly, by its special provisions for schools to be funded directly by central government rather than through the medium of local education authorities. The appeal of all this is unashamedly to self-interest and secular values, and it is a sign of the lack of understanding of what a Catholic school is really a witness to in our society when some prestigious Catholic schools in England have been prepared to seek grant-maintained status at the risk of weakening diocesan educational provision.[18] Mammon before spirit this may be, but it is also a sign of how much the Catholic system of schooling has begun to lose its way and how moribund spiritual leadership seems to have become.

Halsey's research indicated that major determinants of the quality of learning achieved by children in school lay in the nature of the support they received outside of the classroom, in the home, in the church, in the wider social communities to which they belong and in the propensity of such groups to resolve worries and fears which were assuming an exaggerated importance in their lives. In a similar way, the quality of classroom interaction is profoundly affected by the nature of the caring relationship teachers are able to forge with all their pupils and their families. The ability to do this is not easily acquired and yet it is one of the most important aspects of the training of a teacher. Even one of the great philosophical gurus of our day and the darling of the political right in England, Professor Anthony O'Hear was able to declare in 1981 that educators ought not to see themselves as wholly subservient to immediate economic needs.[19] Indeed, he was able to write:

> The academic core of the education system is or should be self-regulating, for what is at issue fundamentally is the pursuit of truth and the development of the human spirit ... it is one thing to say that schools or universities should be aware of the needs of industry: quite another to direct all one's energies and efforts to turning out people trained for work in industry and nothing else. To attempt to do that is to overlook entirely the higher social functions of the school or university. It is also to see pupils in terms of pre-assigned social roles rather than as individuals to be led to make their own choices. Finally, it is to see a particular

27

state of society as something given, rather than as something genuinely free people might wish, at least within the limits of practicability, to alter and reform.[20]

In writing thus about schools, perhaps O'Hear's Jesuit training was coming to the fore while he was unconsciously preparing the epitaph of Margaret Thatcher's educational policy. His views recall a statement of Dom Philip Jebb, made over twenty years ago, that 'all education is the cultivation of awareness and its expression and (thus) Christian awareness is not a superstructure on the natural but is at the heart of life, and by giving natural experience ultimate meaning reveals it for what it is.'[21] After all, the advance of scientific knowledge and the growing sophistication of technology have not brought in their wake acceptable solutions to our moral and spiritual condition.[22] If the Catholic school has failed, it has done so largely because it has succumbed to the values of the industrial, materialistic meritocracy rather than challenged its assumptions and attitudes. This challenging role is what was envisaged in *Gravissimum educationis,* from 'the spirit of Jesus, alive and active in our world today'.[23]

NOTES

1. Philip H. Coombs: *The World Crisis in Education* (Oxford: OUP, 1985), p. 255. This paper is a revised version of the opening paper in *Aspects of Education,* 46, 1992, on 'The Concept of Catholic Education'.
2. *Gravissimum educationis,* 28 October, 1965, reproduced in Austin Flannery: *Vatican Council II: The Conciliar and Post-Conciliar Documents* (Collegeville: The Liturgical Press 1975), p. 729.
3. Ibid., pp. 732-733.
4. The *Catholic Herald,* 5 July 1963. See also my chapter on 'Education (*Gravissimum educationis*)' in Adrian Hastings: *Modern Catholicism: Vatican II and After* (London: SPCK, 1991), pp. 172ff.
5. Quoted from K.L. Woodward: *Making Saints* (London: Chatto & Windus, 1991), pp. 402-403.

6. Ibid., p. 404.
7. *Understanding Christian Nurture* (British Council of Churches, 1981), p. 5.
8. Ibid., p. 100
9. William A. Kopp: *How Persons Grow in Christian Community* (Philadelphia: Fortress Press, 1973), p. 5.
10. Colin Aloes: *The Christian in Education* (SCM Press, London, 1972), pp. 111-112.
11. James Michael Lee: 'Roman Catholic Religious Education' in Marvin J. Taylor: *Foundations for Christian Education in an Era of Change* (Nashville: Abingdon Press, 1976), p. 247.
12. Patrick Kelly: *Catholic Schools,* A briefing for priests, especially those who are governors of schools, 9 December 1987 (R. C. Diocese of Salford, UK), pp. 5-6.
13. Mary Warnock: *Schools of Thought* (London: Faber & Faber, 1977), pp. 132, 135.
14. Pietro Braido: Don Bosco's Pedagogical Experience (Rome: Las, 1989), p. 136.
15. Dudley Plunkett: *Deciding Educational Values: End of the Phoney War?* Occasional Paper No. 25 (Oxford: The Farmington Institute for Christian Studies, 1987), p. 3.
16. Ibid.
17. Ibid.
18. See V.A. McClelland, 'Reflections on a Changing Concept of Teacher Education' in V.A. McClelland and V.P. Varma (eds): *Advances in Teacher Education* (London: Routledge, 1989) pp. 1933.
19. A. O'Hear: Education, Society and Human Nature (London: Routledge & Kegan Paul, 1981) p. 136.
20. Ibid., pp. 136-137.
21. Philip Jebb (ed.) *Religious Education* (London: Darton, Longman & Todd, 1968) p. 6.
22. V.A. McClelland 'An Education for Our Time', *Priests and People,* Vol. I, No. 7, 1987, pp. 275-279.
23. John Callaghan and Michael Cockett: *Are Our Schools Christian? A Call to Pastoral Care* (Great Wakering: Mayhew McCrimmon, 1975), p. 11.

THE ROLE OF THE FAMILY IN EDUCATION: THE IRISH STORY

Aine Hyland

This article addresses the question of the role of the family in education under three headings: firstly, the family as depicted in textbooks in Ireland in the nineteenth and twentieth centuries; secondly, the role of the family, particularly parents, in Irish education during the same period; finally, some current issues relating to the role of parents and the family in education.

In the nineteenth century the Irish national school textbooks contributed to a socially stratified view of Irish society. The lessons of these text books firmly established the social inferiority of the 'poorer classes' of Irish society. Moreover, every opportunity was taken in the lessons of the schoolbooks to inculcate appropriate moral values as well as attitudes of subservience and obedience both within society as a whole and for the children within the home. The first lesson of the third reading book in the 1880s is a particularly good example of this. The following extract is taken from this lesson:[1]

ALL MANKIND, GOD'S FAMILY

See where stands the cottage of the labourer, covered with warm thatch; the mother is spinning at the door; the young children sport before her on the grass; the elder ones learned to labour, and are obedient; the father worketh to provide them food; either he tilleth the ground or gathereth in the corn, or shaketh his ripe apples from the tree; his children run to meet him when he cometh home; and his wife prepareth the wholesome meal.

The father, the mother and the children make a family. The father is the master thereof. If the family be numerous and the grounds large, there are servants to help to do the work: all these dwell in one house; they sleep beneath one roof; they eat the same bread; they kneel down together and praise God every night and every morning with one voice; they are very closely united, and are dearer to each other than any strangers.

Many commentators would argue that this presented a rather idealistic picture of the Irish rural family of the nineteenth century. Nevertheless, it indicates the picture of the Irish family which educational leaders wished to project. A further example of the ideal family situation is presented in this short poem from the second class reader:

Love between Brothers and Sisters

Whatever brawls disturb the street,
There should be peace at home;
Where sisters dwell and brothers meet,
Quarrels should never come.

Birds in their little nests agree;
And 'tis a shameful sight,
When children of one family
Fall out, and chide, and fight.

Hard names at first and threatening words,
That are but noisy breath,
May grow to clubs and naked swords,
To murder and to death.

Pardon, O Lord, our childish rage,
Our little brawls remove;
That as we grow to riper age,
Our hearts may all be love.[2]

Fundamentally, then, the Irish national school readers were used in an attempt to exercise some element of social control over the school-going population and to provide a vision of the type of society which its leaders would have liked to see developing.

The fact that many families were less united and had to strive continually to overcome difficult social conditions was not adverted to in the schoolbooks. However, lessons in the reading books for the senior classes attempted to inculcate a sense of thrift, of the work ethic and of temperance in the young. Both the fourth and fifth readers contained lessons on the danger of strong drink, which were designed to frighten the young people into temperance if nothing else! The following extract from Part I of a lesson in the fourth book in 1891 gives a good indication of the tone of these lessons:

> Young people who begin taking a little beer or spirits because they find it cheers them up for the time are unfortunately often led on to become fond of strong drink and to take too much of it. They become the slaves of drink and get less and less able to govern themselves. They become noisy or silly. They quarrel, or cry, or fight for the smallest cause. Their very faces alter, and they get the miserable look of the regular drunkard. The whole body becomes disordered, from the crown of the head to the sole of the foot, the poison of drink is doing its work. Diseased liver, diseased lungs, diseased heart, diseased brain, these are the fruits of a habit which, when it was begun, was never meant to do any harm.[3]

The setting up of the Temperance Movement in Ireland in the 1890s contributed to the inclusion of lessons such as this in the national schoolbooks. As a result of pressure from this movement, excise duty was imposed on alcoholic liquor in Ireland for the first time in 1891. The monies accruing from this tax were allocated to educational purposes and so we find the ironic situation in the 1890s and early twentieth century that the more drink that was sold, the more additional money was available for national and intermediate education. As the Temperance Movement became more effective at the beginning of the twentieth century, the 'whiskey money' (as it was called) began to dry up. By the end of the first decade of the twentieth century, the proportion of the 'whiskey money' which was made available for intermediate education had virtually disappeared and a new source of funding had to be identified.

In reading the nineteenth and early twentieth century textbooks, one might be forgiven for assuming that Irish family life was uniformly peaceful and untroubled. However, the history of Irish industrial schools and workhouses indicates a very different situation. In the middle of the nineteenth century the total number of children under the age of fifteen in Irish workhouses was 76,700, which represented 6.5% of the total population of that age in Ireland. Of this about fifty thousand were aged between nine and fifteen, sixteen thousand of whom were orphans while a further seventeen thousand had lost one parent.[4] These official figures may not give an entirely accurate account of orphans in the workhouses, since a certain proportion of children registered as orphans were not in fact parentless. Many children had been deserted by their parents during the Famine and had been entered fraudulently, sometimes by the parents themselves, as orphans.

Moreover, widespread desertion of children by parents was common during the distress of the Famine years. In some cases, parents deserted their children when they found themselves unable to provide for them or when they emigrated overseas. In others, children were deserted within the workhouse when their parents absconded from the institution.

The industrial schools which were set up later in the century had two main functions: (i) to provide skills and training to enable children to become self-sufficient in later life, capable of supporting themselves with honest labour; (ii) to mould the characters of children committed to the schools, ensuring that they became decent, law-abiding citizens. In the case of these children there was a conscious effort to separate them from their family and home. When the children entered the industrial school, links between child and home were ruthlessly cut. The breaking of family ties was justified by the belief that children of the destitute and the criminal were in some way predisposed to immorality and crime. The purpose of the schools was to break the cycle of low morals and evil tendencies associated with the lower classes. The policy of separating children from parents was pursued within the Irish industrial school system. Children were usually committed for the maximum period, i.e. until they reached sixteen years of age. As a result, many children spent most of their childhood in an industrial school. They had very little contact with their families. Letters were withheld or censored and visits from parents could only be made with the agreement of the industrial school manager. While the Industrial School Act provided for the option of allowing children to spend a night at home with parents, this option was never in practice exercised because it was believed 'that their parents are generally bad and we generally separate them altogether from their parents'.[5]

The two sides of 'family' can thus be seen from nineteenth-century practice. Children were encouraged to honour and obey their parents within the ideal family but nobody saw any problem in removing children from the influence of what were seen as bad parents.

The picture of Irish family life as depicted in the school textbooks of the new Irish Free State did not differ significantly from that of the nineteenth century. The ideal again was that of a rural, self-sufficient family, obedient children, attending school, working on the family farm, and helping the mother in the home. Textbooks during the first fifty years of the new State have a strongly rural bias and rarely focus on town or city life. Even as recently as the 1960s, the illustrations of the Irish language programme for national schools, based on Buntús Gaeilge, provide a picture of stable nuclear families where mother and father have predetermined roles, with father going out to work and mother staying at home working in the kitchen and looking after the family needs.

This idealised picture of Irish family life was to come under attack in later years by critics who argued that such a picture was no longer an accurate reflection of reality in many parts of Irish society.

The role of parents in Irish education
It is not very difficult to provide an overview of the role of parents in Irish education in the nineteenth and early twentieth centuries. In his detailed analysis of the Irish national school system in the nineteenth century D.H. Akenson asks 'What rights and

prerogatives did the parents of the children have under the national system?' His answer was 'almost none'.[6] His history of nineteenth century Irish national education – *The Irish Education Experiment* – depicts how the system of control and management of national schools had developed so that by the mind-nineteenth century virtually all schools were under the patronage of bishops and were managed by the local priest or clergyman. Akenson maintains that 'the common peasant would have no voice at all in deciding how his children were to be taught and ultimately the only way a parent could express disapproval of the conduct of his local national school was to withdraw his child from education'.[7]

While this is, strictly speaking, true, it would be wrong to suggest that parents never entered the school classroom. During the early decades of the national school system, it was not uncommon for parents to attend at the school when the inspector came to examine the children. The right of parents to enter the classroom was written into the rules for national schools, although these rights were more limited during the period when religious instruction was being given. The rights of parents in relation to their children's religious instruction were also very clearly expressed in the national school rules and parents had a right to withdraw their children from any form of religious instruction of which they did not approve.[8] This right of parents was unambiguous and was introduced to ensure that children were not subjected to proselytism. Apart, however, from this aspect of a child's education there was little or no reference to parents' rights or obligations in the national school rules.

The lack of parental involvement in education was regretted by the resident commissioner of national education, W.J.M. Starkie, in the early twentieth century. Writing in 1902, he stated:

> It is generally admitted that, without the local cooperation of independent and educated lay opinion, the best constructed and best coordinated system in the world is an engine without any driving power; and so to a large extent the whole question of which I have rashly attempted a solution, resolves itself into this: how are we to discover

the independent educated layman or to create him if he does not yet exist?

He found it particularly difficult to identify such a person in the south and he seemed to suggest that it was more difficult to persuade Catholics to become actively involved in their children's education than Protestants. This suggestion was resented by the catholic clergy and the concern of school managers about the issues raised by Starkie led to the setting up of what is now the very effective Catholic Primary School Managers Association. Two years after Starkie wrote his controversial paper, an English HMI, F.H. Dale, visited Ireland and reported on the Irish primary school situation. He also referred to the lack of local interest in Irish education and stated that 'except among the clergy, little or no local interest is manifest in the primary schools in Ireland'.[10] Commenting on this in his book *A Mirror to Kathleen's Face,* D.H. Akenson suggested that the absence of parental and citizen involvement in national schools was probably harmful.[11] In pointing out that schools function most effectively when there is a connection between the home and the school, he maintained that if parents are involved in the school in some way they are more likely to be understanding of the schools' methods and supportive of its objectives, so that the child's experience in school and at home complement each other. The lack of parental involvement and, indeed, of formal structures whereby parents' voices could be heard in Irish education was admitted by An Taoiseach, Eamon De Valera, in 1953. Replying to a query from a New York educator in that year, he stated:

> There are few parents associations as such and parent participation in school activities is, therefore, usually in accordance with the desire of individual parents in this respect. The Constitution of Ireland, however, lays down that the primary rights and responsibilities in education are those of the parents and our system of education is based throughout on this principle.[12]

It is, of course, worth noting that the 1937 Constitution

devotes a full section to the family. Article 41.1.1 states that 'the state recognises the Family as the natural primary and fundamental unit group of society, and as a moral institution possessing inalienable and imprescriptible rights, antecedent and superior to all positive law'. Article 41.1.2 continues: 'The state guarantees to protect the Family in its constitution and authority, as the necessary basis of social order and as indispensable to the welfare of the nation and the state'. In relation to education, Article 42.1 reads: 'the state acknowledges that the primary and natural educator of the child is the Family and guarantees to respect the inalienable right and duty of parents to provide, according to their means, for the religious and moral, intellectual, physical and social education of their children'.[13]

In spite of this clear and unambiguous statement of the rights of the family in education, no formal structures were put in place until the 1970s to enable these rights to be exercised. It was not until after Vatican II in the mid-1960s that the Catholic Church actively supported the setting up of structures whereby control and management of schools might be shared with parents. The role of parents in the education of their children was most articulately stated in the Vatican II *Declaration on Christian Education*:

> Parents who have the first and inalienable duty and right to educate their children should enjoy true freedom in their choice of schools. Consequently public authority which has the obligation to oversee and defend the liberties of citizens, ought to see to it out of concern for distributive justice, that public subsidies are allocated in such a way that, when selecting schools for their children, parents are genuinely free to follow their conscience.[14]

Another Vatican II document, *The Declaration on Religious Freedom,* reiterates the important role of parents in the education of their children. In chapter 1.5 it states:

> Parents, moreover, have the right to determine in accordance with their own religious beliefs, the kind of religious

education their children are to receive. Government, in consequence, must acknowledge the right of parents to a genuine choice of schools and of other means of education.[15]

Partly as a result of the debate which followed Vatican II, parents began to take a more active interest in educational matters. The decision in 1966 by the Minister for Education, Donagh O'Malley, to introduce free second-level education was a watershed in Irish education. Already the state had taken a more direct role in the provision of post-primary education by the setting up of comprehensive schools in a limited number of areas. In the late 1960s there was considerable debate about the future of second-level education, and the question of rationalisation, amalgamation, etc. was a live one in many areas. Public meetings were held by the Department of Education in a number of centres around the country with a view to presenting their plans for second-level education. These meetings elicited considerable public interest and were attended by a very large numbers of parents. In 1969 the Minister for Education, Brian Lenihan, issued a booklet entitled *All Our Children* to every household in the country. This booklet was for parents and its purpose was to give them as briefly as possible the basic facts about the education of their children. In his introduction, the Minister referred to the great change that was taking place in Irish education; he spoke about the considerably increased investment that the government was making in education and reiterated the government's commitment to 'our most urgent social and educational objective: equality of opportunity'. He recognised the importance of the parents' role in education, stating that 'it is essential that parents understand the structure of Irish education and particularly that they know when and how to make those crucial decisions on which to a great extent their children's future depends'. He concluded 'that is why this booklet has been compiled and is being sent to every household in Ireland'.[16]

The 1970s was an interesting decade in Irish education from the point of view of the parental role. By the beginning of the decade, there was a number of parent associations in individual schools around the country and at least two national parent associations were set up. One of these was the Parent School Movement, whose spokesperson was Yvonne McGrath. The Parent School Movement became involved in a number of the debates on education which took place during the early 1970s. Another parent organisation which was vocal during those years was the Federation of Parents' Associations which represented parent-teacher associations of national schools under Protestant management. Among the issues raised by this federation was the question of access by Protestant parents to free secondary education and the federation campaigned for the setting up of Protestant comprehensive schools. This organisation also called for greater involvement by parents in the running of national schools.[17]

In June 1973 Sean O Connor, Secretary of the Department of Education, spoke at the Annual Conference of the Catholic Primary Schools Managers Association in Athlone and he made the first official reference in public to the possibility of shared management of the national schools. In the course of this talk he said:

> Parents have no say at all in the management of the school. I know there are advisory committees. I'm talking about authority. Yet their children are being educated in the schools and both before God and before the Constitution they are responsible. I think it would be politic to share that responsibility.[18]

Within two years agreement had been reached between the Department of Education and school patrons on the setting up of boards of management in national schools. Broadly speaking it was agreed that the boards of management would consist of representatives of the patrons, elected parents and the principal teacher, and an elected teacher in larger schools. The actual constitution of the board varied according to the size of school, but in all cases the patrons' nominees formed a majority on the board. The patrons also nominated the chairperson of the board – in virtually all cases the local parish priest or rector. Boards of management of national schools came into being in 1975 and within a year virtually every national school had set up a board. The speed by which this transformation occurred was in no small measure related to the fact that the new and increased capitation grant for national schools would be paid by the department only if a board of management was in place.

Much has been written in recent years about the growth of parent associations and parent councils in schools. It has been suggested that the decision in 1985 by the Minister for Education, Gemma Hussey, to set up a National Parents Council was a top down imposition and did not reflect the interests of parents at grassroots level. I cannot agree with this suggestion. I have already referred to the existence of at least two national parent groups, and by the late 1970s elected parents on boards of management had also set up a further body entitled the Council for Parents' Elected Representatives on National Schools' Boards of Management. This Council existed for at least five years from 1977 to 1982 and only faded out when the CPSMA extended its terms of reference to enable elected parents to take an active role in that association.[19] The decision by Minister Hussey in 1985 to provide a seeding grant for a National Parents' Council and to set out structures for the two tiers of the council (primary and post-primary) was a very important decision. The National Parents' Council has been remarkably successful in focusing and projecting the voices of parents and this has been particularly true since the publication of the Green Paper on Education in 1992. Both groups published a detailed response to the Green Paper and the National Parents' Council – Primary opened the debate in Dublin Castle at the National Education Convention in October 1993, with what was generally recognised as an outstanding presentation. The issues raised in this presentation provide the basis for the next and final section of this paper.

Current issues relating to the role of parents and the family in education

I have referred earlier in this paper to the rights of parents in relation to their children's education, as enshrined in the 1937 Constitution. The National Parents' Council argues that the forthcoming educational legislation which has been promised by successive Ministers must articulate principles which will permeate the content and processes of the statute.[20] They maintain that these principles must enshrine and reflect the fundamental provision of the Constitution on education which acknowledges the family as the primary and natural educator of the child and guarantees to respect the inalienable right and duty of parents to provide for the religious and moral, intellectual, physical and social education of their children. This right, they state, has been defined as one that cannot be transferred or given away. It accords to parents fundamental status and natural law rights, as primary decision-makers in the matter of their children's education. Thus, they maintain, the legislative framework deriving from the Constitution must incorporate the principles of participation, parents' right to be heard, and their right to be supported as agents of their children's learning.

The inalienable right and duty of parents in the matter of their children's education is supported by the teaching of many churches. For example, it is powerfully set out in an encyclical of the Catholic Church, *Gravissimum educationis,* which notes that the gravest obligation rests with families for children's education, an obligation which requires that they be recognised as primarily and principally responsible for that education. However, while recognising that such a strong statement could support the claim of parents for control within the educational system, the National Parents Council did not put forward such a case. What they have asked for is real partnership, teamwork and active sharing of responsibility at all levels. They are not prepared to settle for 'a little partnership here and an involvement there'. They are adamant that 'either the ethos of shared responsibility on equal terms permeates the process, or it is some other principle which underpins the educational decision-making processes. Partnership and dominance cannot co-exist.'

It was in this context that Minister for Education Niamh Bhreathnach attempted to reconcile the wishes of parents and teachers for 'real partnership' when she issued the position paper on *The Management and Governance of Schools* in summer 1994. [21] This paper attempted to come up with a framework and structure which would satisfy both the school owners/patrons/trustees and parents and teachers. The formula suggested was one whereby parents and teachers would suggest names for inclusion in an expanded board of management and the Patron would formally nominate these if they were acceptable to him/her. However, by the end of September it was clear that this formula satisfied nobody and we now await the publication of the White Paper on Education to see how the issue of parent partnership in the control and governance of schools can be reconciled with the insistence of the Churches that as owners they must remain a majority on the boards of management.

Conclusion

The past 150 years has seen many changes in Irish education. From the middle of the nineteenth to the middle of the twentieth century there appeared to be no alternative to the system whereby the Churches acted in *loco parentis* as far as the control and governance of schools was concerned.

However, as the Irish people became better educated and more vocal they began to claim a more direct role in school management at both primary and post-primary levels. The setting up of boards of management of national schools in 1975 was the first breakthrough for parental involvement. The setting up of a National Parents Council in 1985 provided a further opportunity for parents to strengthen their involvement in their children's education. From the mid-1980s onwards, voluntary secondary schools also began to set up boards of management – particularly those schools run by religious orders. At present, about 75 per cent of secondary schools have boards of management. Where parents have been given a role in the running of schools they have contributed responsibly and constructively. By and large, they have worked with teacher unions on issues which affect children's lives in schools – they have campaigned on class size, levels of current and capital grants and other such issues. In general, parents recognise the demanding and responsible task facing teachers and have worked with them rather than against them at both local and national level. It is important that this partnership between parents and teachers continues because when parents become vocal in a general criticism of teachers and the school system, political responses are not always the best. Recent examples in countries such as France and the UK are not encouraging in relation to changes introduced by governments at the apparent behest of parents. In this regard, it is important that those parents who are content and satisfied with their children's schooling should play a full role in their local parents council or school board of management and not allow a situation to develop whereby only disaffected parents become active and vocal. We are fortunate in this country that so many committed and interested parents are willing to play a role in the structures which are now available within the school system, i.e. parents councils and boards of management. British Prime Minister Winston Churchill once said that 'the price of freedom is eternal vigilance'. Parents who are interested in their children's education should remember this and should avail of the opportunities which are now there for playing a fuller role.

NOTES

1. Commissioners of National Education, *Third Reading Book* (Dublin: 1885).
2. Commissioners of National Education, *Second Reading Book* (Dublin: 1883).
3. Commissioners of National Education, *Fourth Reading Book* (Dublin: 1891).
4. Jane Barnes, *Irish Industrial Schools 1868-1908* (Dublin: Irish Academic Press, 1989), p. 12.
5. Ibid., pp. 89-90.
6. D.H. Akenson, *The Irish Education Experiment* (London: 1970), pp. 154-55.
7. Ibid.
8. Commissioners of National Education, *Rules for National Schools* (Dublin: Stationery Office, 1898).
9. W.J.M. Starkie, *Recent Reforms in Irish Education, Primary and Secondary, with a view to their Co-ordination* (Dublin: J. M. Blackie, 1902), pp. 38-9.
10. F.H. Dale, *Report on Primary Education in Ireland 1904,* quoted in Aine Hyland and K. Milne, *Irish Educational*

Documents Vol. 1 (Dublin: CICE) 1987.

11. D.H. Akenson, *A Mirror to Kathleen's Face* (Montreal and London: McGill-Queen's University Press, 1975), pp. 4-5.

12. Quoted in S. O'Buachalla, *Education Policy in Twentieth Century Ireland* (Dublin: Wolfhound Press, 1988), p. 320.

13. *Bunreacht na hEireann* (Dublin: 1937).

14. *Declaration on Christian Education(Gravissimum educationis)* quoted in W. Abbott, *Documents of Vatican II* (London-Dublin: 1966), p.637.

15. *Declaration on Religious Freedom(Dignitatis humanae),* quoted in Abbott, op. cit., p.675.

16. B. Lenihan, *All Our Children* (Dublin: Department of Education, 1969).

17. The minute books and some papers of the Federation of Parents' Associations are in the possession of the author.

18. Sean O'Connor, Address to the Annual Conference of the CPSMA, June 1973.

19. Some of the reports and papers of the Council for Parents' Elected Representatives on National Schools' Boards of Management are in the possession of the author.

20. This section summarises the points made by the National Parents' Council – Primary in its presentation to the National Education Convention in October: 1993.

21. N. Bhreathnach, *The Management and Governance of Schools* (Dublin: Department of Education, 1994).

THE FUTURE OF CATHOLIC
SECOND-LEVEL SCHOOLS IN IRELAND

J. Matthew Feheney FPM

One of the aspects of the theme of this book, *Education and the Family*, of special interest to many Catholic parents, is the future of Catholic post-primary or second-level schools. I will look at the future of these schools, but my treatment of the topic will in no way seek to be definitive: there are so many imponderables at the moment that it is extremely difficult to say with any confidence what the medium- and long-term future will bring for these schools. My hope is, nevertheless, that this paper will encourage further discussion of the topic and will, in due course, lead to a clarification of the issues involved.

Broadly speaking, there are three types of Catholic second-level school in Ireland: firstly, a small number of voluntary secondary schools under lay trustees; secondly, a larger number of comprehensive and community schools, the governance structure of which differs from that of voluntary secondary schools. The number of Catholic community schools is far greater than the number of Catholic comprehensive schools, the latter being an experiment that ceased with the arrival of the more popular community schools. Finally, there is the largest group of all, the Catholic voluntary secondary schools, whether single-sex or co-educational. There are two sub-divisions in this group, the larger number being under the trusteeship of religious congregations. The second section is made up of a small number of what were formerly junior seminaries, originally catering for boys only, under diocesan trustees, but now operating as voluntary secondary schools, opening their doors to the students, though not in every case to the girls, in their area. I wish to concentrate exclusively on Catholic voluntary secondary schools under the trusteeship of religious congregations.

The imminent prospect of a White Paper on Education, and the increasing rate of the withdrawal of religious personnel from voluntary secondary schools, has caused many people to wonder about their long-term future. The large number of these schools and demand for places in them, which is an indication of the high regard in which they are held by parents, would suggest that their future is of great concern to a large number of people in this country. In 1994 there were 225,968 students in 453 voluntary secondary schools, the majority of them under the trusteeship of religious congregations.[1]

The disappearance of religious from schools

Twenty years ago most of these schools had a religious as principal and about half the teaching staff were also religious. In 1963 only three per cent of the principals of these schools were lay.[2] Since then there has been a steady decline in the number of religious both in the post of principal and on the teaching staff. In 1994 almost half the principals in these schools were lay as also were 80 per cent of the teaching staff.[3] All the indications are that the number of religious will continue to fall and that, within ten years, religious will virtually have disappeared from these schools.

Nor must it be thought that the Church has not foreseen this. In a document issued in 1988 the Vatican Congregation for Christian Education expressed its willingness to hand over the direction of the schools it had established to lay people, though it gave warning that the recognition of any school as Catholic was reserved to the 'competent ecclesiastical authority'.[4] This, however, is merely a restatement of a provision in the new *Code of Canon Law.*

I think that the majority, if not all of the lay principals of schools under the trusteeship of religious congregations are people of outstanding character, commitment and professionalism. Any questions I raise here are not by way of querying either the commitment of these lay people, or the success they have made of their jobs. My main concerns in this paper are trends, policies and large-scale effects. It is also relevant to remark that most of these lay principals were chosen, almost hand-picked, because they were already well-known for their commitment to the ideals of Catholic education and, in many cases also, for their commitment to the ethos of the congregation whose members are the trustees of that particular school. So, let it be clearly understood that, in this article, I am concerned with policies rather than personalities and with the future rather than the present.

It would probably be true to say that, in the face of decreasing numbers, the strategy being adopted by religious congregations in Ireland to ensure that the founding ethos prevails in those schools now under lay principals and staffs is the establishment of effective boards of management. Trustees feel that, by retaining a majority on the board, together with the power to nominate the chairperson, they will be able to ensure that the school will remain Catholic and will continue to promote and be guided by Gospel values. The present formula for the appointment of members of boards of management of voluntary secondary schools is: two members nominated by the teaching staff, two members nominated by the parents, three members, in addition to the chairperson, nominated by the trustees. The principal is a non-voting member and acts as secretary to the board.

For the privilege of being trustees, the particular religious congregation has to accept ultimate legal and financial responsibility for the school. This is not to say that the majority of salaries and capital costs do not come from the Government: only that the trustees have to pick up the tab for any shortfalls and are ultimately liable in the event of litigation.

As long as the religious congregation remains a viable entity, there seems to be no good reason why it should not be able to discharge its responsibilities as trustee. This is not to say that it will be able to provide members, or even chairpersons, for the board of management of each school from the ranks of its own religious personnel. In fact, the majority of the trustee nominees to boards of management, and, increasingly, even the chairpersons, are lay people. The appointment of lay people to represent the trustees raises its own problems. The trustees have an obligation to ensure that the institutions operating in their name practise and promote values in accordance with their own philosophy and mission statement.

But if lay people, acting in the name of the congregation, are faithfully to represent the values of the congregation, they will need to receive special training. And this, to be effective, will need to be systematic and ongoing. Though this training is important, it is not always regarded as urgent. Consequently, as in other areas of human endeavour, what is deemed urgent gets priority and what is often, in the long run, much more important, can get neglected. Perhaps the solution may be for each congregation to have a general rule to the effect that they will have ongoing training for their trustee nominees on boards and that only those who have completed a designated orientation course will be selected for this responsibility.

The problem of obtaining trustee nominees for boards of management can also constitute a logistical problem for a congregation with many schools. Under present arrangements, the board for each school will require three trustee nominees, apart from the chairperson. Ten schools will require thirty nominees. Some congregations, such as the Christian Brothers, have up to two hundred schools, between primary and secondary, in Ireland. These schools require up to six hundred trustee representatives, each group serving a three-year term. So the training process has to begin anew every three years. The problem of providing training and servicing, including what might be termed pastoral care, for such a large number of people can, therefore, be a considerable challenge. But who is to deny that it is an important one and, ultimately, a wonderful means of empowering people and developing their leadership talents for use in Catholic education!

Options for the future

The strategy of using the board of management to ensure that the congregational values are the values that guide and inform the school depends for its success on the religious congregation retaining sufficient vigour and energy so that it is able either to supply its own personnel for boards of management or train lay people to represent them adequately. If, as seems likely, vocations continue to decline at the present rate, a stage will be reached by the majority of congregations involved in voluntary secondary schools in Ireland where they will not be able to do the former. The latter, that is training lay people to represent them, will then assume even greater importance, not only for the sake of the influence of the particular congregation but for the sake of the teachers, students and parents who want to see the distinctive ethos of a particular school continue.

If, however, a particular congregation became so depleted that it was unable, even with the help of lay people, to continue to discharge its duties as trustees, what is likely to happen to the governance of the particular school? If that particular school is to survive, it would be necessary to transfer the trusteeship to another suitable body. There are at least three possibilities here: another religious congregation, the diocese and the Department of Education.

Transferring the trusteeship to another religious congregation is not a likely long-term alternative because the reason for the inability of one congregation to continue to discharge its responsibilities as trustee, namely lack of vocations, is simultaneously operating against other congregations also. The problem of any one congregation is the problem of each of them, the only difference being the degree to which each one is affected. This alternative, therefore, is severely limited in its possibilities.

Another solution lies in rationalisation of the provision of schooling at local level through closure and amalgamation. This has happened in several areas: a school operated by a religious congregation has closed and the pupils have transferred to another, sometimes a VEC school in the area. Amalgamation is the more likely choice when neither of the schools is willing to close. Often a convenient solution is the construction of a new community school, under the Department of Education, or a community college, under the local VEC. One or other of these alternatives will account for the disappearance in the future of some second-level schools now under the trusteeship of religious congregations. This is not to say, however, that there is any desire to terminate an existing connection with any particular religious congregation, as long as it is able and willing to participate in the governance of a particular school. In the case of community schools, for example, the responsibilities of trustees are shared between different groups such as the diocese, one or more religious congregations and the VEC. It is obvious that the burden of trusteeship in a partnership arrangement like this is less onerous than that of the normal voluntary secondary school in which the religious congregation is the sole trustee.

Diocesan involvement

The third alternative is the possibility of the transfer to the diocese of the trusteeship of a school now under a religious congregation. This is an alternative on which I would like to reflect in greater detail. It raises the question of the ability and readiness of the Irish diocesan Church to become further involved in second-level education.

The present involvement of the diocesan Church in Ireland in second-level schooling began in the second half of the nineteenth century. The reason was for this involvement was a need to provide candidates for the diocesan priesthood with an adequate preparation for the entrance examinations to the seminaries of the period, especially the national seminary of St Patrick's College, Maynooth, established in 1795. For this purpose post-primary residential schools were established in most dioceses, where students followed the curriculum of the period, including Latin and Greek. After the establishment of the Intermediate Board of Education in 1878, the students sat for the intermediate Board examinations, and, after passing these examinations, or the Matriculation of the National University of Ireland, entered one of the major seminaries. To distinguish them from major seminaries, which were third-level institutions, and in keeping with custom on the continent, the diocesan second-level residential schools came to be called junior seminaries.

The diocesan junior seminaries were, therefore, established for the express purpose of preparing young men for admission to the senior seminary. This involvement gave the diocesan priesthood a limited interest and experience in second-level schooling but it is doubtful if it would predispose this ageing group to take on additional responsibility for another group of schools. The diocesan clergy are already burdened with involvement in parish primary schools. It is extremely unlikely that they would wish to take on responsibility for the trusteeship of another large group of voluntary secondary schools, many of which have little or no direct connection with the diocese, and which, apart from the opportunity to serve, promise little in the way of gain but much in the way of hassle.

Diocesan clergy, therefore, far from welcoming new responsibility for the trusteeship of voluntary secondary schools which have no direct connection with the diocese, are more likely to question the continuation of their involvement in former junior seminaries which are now only marginally, if at all, occupied to any significant extent with what was formerly their chief purpose, and for which they were originally established, namely to prepare boys for entrance to major seminaries. And let it not be forgotten that trusteeship of any school entails acceptance of ultimate financial and legal responsibility.

It should also be noted that the diocesan Church, whether in Ireland or abroad, has traditionally had little direct involvement in second-level schools. It has usually been content to leave this to the religious orders and congregations, who specialised in education. Here we mention in passing only a few of these: Jesuits, Dominicans, Augustinians, Franciscans, Holy Ghost, Marists, as well as the many congregations of teaching brothers and sisters, especially the followers of Edmund Rice, in whose honour and memory this book of essays was planned. Teaching is a specialised work, requiring not only preparation but also aptitude and dedication. The work of the diocesan clergy, on the other hand, is essentially pastoral: celebrating Mass, catechising, evangelising and administering the sacraments, preaching the Word of God, providing spiritual direction, as well as managing and administering diocesan property.

Involving the laity

While, as I have said above, lay people are increasingly being asked to act as trustee nominees on boards of management, there seems to have been little attempt to involve them as trustees, or, even, to permit them to share some of the duties of trusteeship. The general pattern in ecclesiastical affairs in the past has been to give the laity responsibility only when the clergy cannot avoid it. Thus, it is now taken for granted that lay people will be involved in legal and financial affairs, because this is an area requiring specialised knowledge and expertise. The Church of Ireland might provide an example here: it began by sharing responsibility for legal and financial matters but, as the numbers and energy of clergy went down, the services of the laity were availed of in other areas: to represent the Church on committees and in matters of public relations, in producing Church literature, as well as audio and video tapes. The diocesan Catholic Church is gradually following this pattern and there seems to be no good reason why religious congregations cannot follow.

It should be noted here that some religious congregations are experimenting with a greater sharing of their charism and ministry with lay people. One example of this is the lay associate movement. Quite a number of religious congregations have invited these lay associates to live out in their lives the charism and spirituality of the founder of the congregation to which they are attached. Many of these associates are already connected with the work and ministries of the individual religious congregations and, in the case of teaching congregations, some are teachers. There is no reason why these associates, if given the required spiritual and professional training would not be able to assume at least some of the duties of trustees and continue to provide leadership in Catholic education. For this, of course, ongoing, carefully planned formation and training in leadership would be necessary.

These associates might be regarded as the modern equivalent of the older Third Order groups. Many congregations now have these associate groups, which meet regularly for prayer, liturgy, study and discussion.

Other groups capable of similar dedication and loyalty are parents, teachers and past pupils. All they need is training and development and the opportunity to use their talents and gifts. Built into the training, of course, would be safety procedures and rules: the normal checks and balances to ensure that trust is not abused and the interests, welfare and future of others thereby jeopardised.

The time has come to involve the laity much more in every aspect of the life and ministry of the Church. No doubt the reason why the official Church does not make more use of their talents is not unconnected with the perception, if not fact, that it was, in the past, and still continues to be hierarchical and clerically dominated to a marked degree. This, however, has not always been the case: the founder of the first Church school in Alexandria in 202 was Origen, an eighteen-year-old layman, to whom we shall return again below. Dermot Lane, in advocating the fostering of lay ownership and responsibility for Catholic schools, gives us a timely reminder that some of the most outstanding pioneers in Irish Catholic education were lay people, including Edmund Rice, Nano Nagle, Catherine McAuley and Margaret Aylward.[5]

The vision of the Catholic school

At present throughout the world there are about 150,000 Catholic schools with more than forty million students. There is no sign of the disappearance of Catholic schools in the free world: the demand for them continues. Stated in broad terms, the purpose of the Catholic school is an attractive challenge: 'it is based on an educational philosophy in which faith, culture and life are brought into harmony.'[6] The most recent document from the Vatican, *The Religious Dimension of Education in a Catholic School* (1988),[7] provides an inspiring vision of Catholic education at its best. It is, moreover, a broad and generous involvement in the transmission of culture, not merely in narrow catechising and evangelising.

Nearly thirty years ago Vatican II stated in its *Declaration on Christian Education* that 'the Catholic school pursues cultural goals and the natural development of youth to the same degree as any other school.' It went on to say that what makes a Catholic school distinctive is its attempt to generate a community climate in the school that was permeated by the Gospel spirit of freedom and love.[8] Few would find fault with these sentiments. Unfortunately, in the living out of them, there is often a regrettable narrowness not in keeping with the stated ideal. It is important at this critical stage in the history of Catholic second-level schools to remember that, throughout its long history, the nearer the Catholic school has come to living out Gospel values the nearer it has come to making people truly free. The word 'liberal' does not accurately describe the freedom which the following of Gospel values confers on people, but it does convey something of its true spirit. One the other hand, the further the Catholic school has departed from Gospel values, the more it has become turned in on itself, the narrower its focus and the less it has fulfilled the promise of Jesus to set people free (Jn 8:32).

Throughout the history of the Catholic Church there has always been a tradition of openness to other cultures in Catholic education which, in the tradition of Jesus of Nazareth, welcomed dialogue with different cultures and sought to examine and appreciate their richness in the light of faith. This tradition has, however, often been a minority one, espoused only by individuals or small groups. But it is, none the less, a valid tradition. On the other hand, opposed to this open approach, has been another tradition: one which viewed other cultures with suspicion, even antagonism. These two opposing views can be seen very clearly in the Church as early as the beginning of the third century, one exemplified by Origen and the other by Tertullian. I shall look at these two proponents of the two opposing views in some detail because I believe that they are prototypes of an ongoing tension, which is as much alive today as ever. I shall draw attention later to an example of the very same debate now in progress in England. But first, I will look at the third century Church's involvement in education.

A heritage of eighteen centuries

In the early Church, Christians who took their faith seriously saw to it that no one was admitted to their company without careful instruction in the faith and appropriate examination to determine the result. Thus *catechesis,* or religious instruction, was recognised by the early Church as one of its major obligations. What is generally regarded as the first school officially under the direction of the Church was Origen's Catechetical School in Alexandria. [9]

In the year 202 Demetrius, Bishop of Alexandria, placed the eighteen-year-old Origen in charge of catechesis in his diocese. Initially Origen taught the elements of Christian doctrine to catechumens preparing for baptism. After some time, however, he encountered men who wished to be Christians and who had already studied at the famous Museum at Alexandria. Their philosophy raised questions about God and immortality, about the nature of morality and other problems in Greek philosophy. Origen, therefore, reorganised his *catechesis,* incorporating it into the organisational structure of a *didaskaleion,* or typical Greek school of the period, and embarked upon a new course.[10]

Origen had two levels of education in his new programme. He put his average students through a four-year course which was the usual education for free-born Greek youths. It included grammar, rhetoric, logic, arithmetic, geometry (including some geography and rudimentary biology), astronomy (including what was known of physics) and music. This first level of education was a preparation for the second level which involved the study of philosophy. Origen introduced his abler and more brilliant students to the study of the great philosophic questions of the time: the nature of truth; whether there was 'one river of Truth'; whether the Logos, Wisdom of the Greeks, was not the same as the inspiration that had burst upon the Jewish Prophets and had become incarnate as the Word, Jesus Christ.[11]

One of Origen's pupils, Gregory of Neocaesarea, described his introductory course in philosophy as follows:

> He introduced us to all schools of thought and was determined that we should be ignorant of no type of Greek doctrine …nothing was forbidden us, nothing hidden from us, nothing inaccessible to us.[12]

Origen's willingness to assimilate what he considered the best in Greek culture in the third century was not, however, representative of the attitude of Christians as a whole. The general feeling would appear to have been a rejection of this culture. It has been suggested, however, that the Christian uneasiness about, and even rejection of the culture of the Roman and Hellenistic world was a rejection only of a particular culture, the values of which did not appeal to Christians, because it answered few of their needs. The rejection, in so far as it was that, did not imply a rejection of all culture. Even in the case of Origen, however, there were two significant features of his school which would appear to be characteristic of the Church's assimilation and acceptance of all the subsequent cultures which she encountered. The first of these features was selectivity. Gregory of Neocaesarea stated that there was one philosophical school of thought that Origen advised his pupils not to explore: this was the Epicurean School. The reason given was that, as the Epicureans were atheists, they had no answers to the questions a Christian might ask and they asked no questions that a Christian had not already answered. The second feature was that Origen himself was at the side of his young philosophers, directing them, pointing out 'all that was true and useful, putting aside all that was false'. This second feature we might characterise as guidance.[13]

These two features, selectivity and guidance, have always been part of the tradition of the Church in education. But, it could be contended that, in its ordinary implementation, this approach is, in most cases, no more directive, and, in many much less, than that associated with any other similar group. Compare the Catholic approach to education with that of the Japanese, Muslims, orthodox Jews, modern Christian sects among many: the Catholic approach, apart from a minority of conservative and fundamentalist Catholic groups, is liberal by comparison.

But let us return to Origen. It is clear from the above that he was representative of an attitude of openness towards culture and education in the early Church. There were others, equally famous, who shared his view: Justin Martyr (d.163), Origen's teacher, Clement of Alexandria (150-c.215); Eusebius (c.260-c.340); and the most famous of them all, Augustine of Hippo (354-430). Augustine strove for a synthesis between classical learning, especially the philosophy of Plato, and Christianity. He wrote:

> If those who are called philosophers, and especially the Platonists, have said aught that is true and in harmony with our Faith, we are not only not to shrink from it, but to claim it for our own use from those who have unlawful possession of it.[14]

Tertullian of Carthage (155-245) was, however, representative of another attitude towards education within the Church.

Tertullian was a fiery opponent of any synthesis between Greek culture and Christianity. He asked stridently:

> What is there in common between Athens and Jerusalem? What between the *Academy* and the Church? What between heretics and Christians? Away with all projects for a Stoic, a Platonic, a dialectic Christianity. After Jesus Christ, we desire no subtle theories, no acute enquiries after the Gospel.[15]

Tertullian was, therefore, representative of another group within the Church that viewed other cultures with varying degrees of suspicion and fear. Dialogue with the world, for them, was a challenge scarcely worth the trouble and risk. Christian education for them had a narrower focus: to meet the needs of the members of the Church rather than to engage in a dialogue with the world; to instruct its members in the tenets of its own religion rather than to offer to share insights into the mysteries of life and death with others not of the fold; to defend their own beliefs against sceptics and unbelievers rather than take a risk in establishing the Kingdom of God on earth.

The striving for excellence, towards which Catholic schools were always urged in the past, was not without its own theological problems. Some Catholic writers even saw the good Catholic school as eventually defeating its purpose if that purpose is conceived purely in terms of serving the Church only. In the pursuit of the perfect education, as conceived in the twentieth century, such a Catholic school might become more and more liberal and might conceivably arrive at the conclusion that the pursuit of knowledge and intellectual training are worthy of attention for their own sake.[16] But this is unlikely to happen if the school community is committed to Gospel values. I again repeat the distinction between the freedom to which Jesus called people (Jn 8:32) and a liberalism that is equated with the absence of Christian values.

I would, moreover, suggest that a school mission statement, drawn up by the entire staff working with the board of management, and regularly revised, would ensure that the school articulated its core values, which, it is reasonable to assume, will comprise, wholly or in part, Gospel values. Mission statements, which have only recently made their appearance in schools, can be a great help in reminding not only principals and staffs, but also parents and boards of management, of the core values as well as the aims and objectives of their institutions.

If Vatican II brought us back to the vision of the Catholic school that inspired people like Origen and Augustine, there are echoes of the attitude of Tertullian discernible in the stance taken by the Board of Governors in a recent prominent case in England. This is the controversy about the future of St Philip's Sixth Form School in Birmingham, in which the trustees, priests of the Birmingham Oratory, on the one hand, and teachers, parents and students, on the other, took opposing sides. The facts of the case given here are taken from reports in the press and have not been disputed by either side.

In closing months of 1993 the Oratorian Fathers decided to close St Philip's College in Birmingham on the grounds that it was no longer viable as a Catholic institution since the number of Catholic students had fallen to 19 per cent. This, they said, would not be in accord with the College's trust deed. Many parents and staff, however, argued that the college should, none the less, remain a Catholic establishment. After prolonged discussions, much lobbying of and by local politicians, followed by a Government inquiry, the trustees announced in December 1994 that they would terminate the lease for the College in June 1996.

The Oratorian trustees said that, according to their understanding of the College's trust deed, the education provided by the College 'should, on the whole, be by Roman Catholics for Roman Catholics'.[17]

Against a background of misunderstandings between the governors and College staff, the final trigger for the Department of Education and Science (DES) inquiry came when the chairman of the governors, the Oratorian Father Guy Nicholls, suspended the Principal, Edward Picardo, following a dispute over the manner of appointing a new member of staff. The Principal took the view that the post should be advertised. It is understood that Fr Guy Nicholls took a different approach. This, however, was only one of a series of incidents in which Principal and staff were at odds with the governors. Another was the celebration of Mass.

The Oratorians are reported to have threatened disciplinary action if other Catholic priests were invited to say Mass at the school or to lead retreats, which had been a popular feature. In November 1994 campaigners who wanted to preserve St Philip's College as a Catholic institution held a torchlight demonstration outside the home of the Archbishop of Birmingham, Dr Maurice Couve de Murville. They also presented a petition of ten thousand names to support their request that the College remain open. On 20 September the Prefect of the Vatican Congregation for Catholic Education, Cardinal Pio Laghi, pointed out that it was the Archbishop who had responsibility for the College. But the Cardinal added, 'We are convinced that His Grace shares our earnest hope that St Philip's will not be closed. The Congregation for Catholic Education does not wish any Catholic school to be closed and even less one which enjoys such a long and outstanding educational tradition as St Philip's.'[18]

A report commissioned by the Department of Education and Science, while criticising the trustees and the governors for mismanagement, points out that the central issue was the 'Catholicity' of the College. It concluded that while the governors may or may not have been right in pursuing their aims, they did so 'in a totally inappropriate and high-handed manner'. As a result, the governors 'failed to persuade the staff of what they were trying to achieve and also failed to take proper account of the genuine concerns and feelings of the staff...Certainly such attempts as were made to re-establish Catholicity failed in their aims and were … badly mismanaged.'[19]

While contesting the parts of the report which accuse the governors of mismanagement, the Oratorian trustees repeated that their decision to close the famous Birmingham College was 'because of the tenuous connection now remaining with the original Catholicity of the trusts'. The matter of continuing St Philip's as a Catholic College under diocesan trustees is to be taken up with the Archbishop of Birmingham, Dr Maurice Couve de Murville.[20]

I would like to select a few key issues from the St Philip's School case because they illustrate some points which I consider of crucial importance. The first is Cardinal Pio Laghi's statement that 'the Congregation for Catholic Education does not wish any Catholic school to be closed'. In the eyes of the Vatican Congregation, the fact that the number of Catholic students in St Philip's fell to 19 per cent did not justify the closure of a Catholic school, much less one that, in Pio Laghi's words, 'enjoys such a long and outstanding educational tradition'. This statement may come as a surprise to many people, especially those who take the narrower view of a Catholic school: that it exists only for the education of members of the Catholic faith. One can, however, see that Pio Laghi's statement is merely implementing what was stated in 1988 by the Vatican Congregation for Catholic Education: 'Not all students in Catholic schools are members of the Catholic Church; not all are Christian. There are, in fact, countries in which the vast majority of the students are not Catholics.'[21]

Pio Laghi is also to be commended for reminding us of one aspect of the great missionary tradition of the Catholic Church: this is to bring the benefit of education to the different nations and peoples. This was the tradition of the great Christian educators: of Cyril and Methodius; of Columba and Columbanus; of Anselm and Bede; of the great Jesuit educators of the east; Mateo Ricci in Japan and China; of the Irish missionaries to West Africa during the first half of this century. It is the living out of Christ's command to go and teach all nations (Mt 28:18).

The second point concerns the teaching staff of a Catholic school. Implicit in the importance we, in Ireland, assign to boards of management of schools, and the people like the Oratorian trustees of St Philip's, in England, to their board of governors, is the belief that boards of management, or boards of governors, are a crucial means of influencing the ethos of a school: whether it will, for instance, be truly Catholic or merely so in name. This, however, is a belief not universally shared. On the other hand, a good deal of opinion would regard the principal and teaching staff as the single most important determining factor in the ethos of a school (see O'Keeffe and Feheney in this volume p. 00). Again, the Vatican Congregation seems to feel this way for it states that 'prime responsibility for creating this unique Christian school climate rests with the teachers as individuals and as a community'.[22] The same point is put even more forcibly in the Vatican document *Lay Catholics in Schools* (1982), which states unambiguously, 'It is the lay teachers ... believers or not, who will substantially determine whether or not a school realises its aims and accomplishes its objectives.'[23]

Many of our Catholic schools nowadays have a mission statement, and even where they do not, their trustees have a statement of philosophy of education: full of admirable sentiments and worthy aspirations. The trouble, however, is the congruence between the avowed mission statements and practice on the ground. Perhaps this is an aspect of the Irish condition Joe Lee characterises as mistaking the word for the deed. But this is a point, which, owing to lack of space, I am unable to develop further: it would require a separate paper, one which, perhaps, is long overdue.

In this article I suggested that voluntary Catholic second-level schools in Ireland will pass through a critical period during the coming ten years. Like any crisis, however, this can also be a time of great opportunity: especially a time when we affirm our faith in the Catholic school true to Gospel values; a time also when we show our confidence in the laity, the people of God, and give them the opportunity to play their full part in continuing the best traditions of Catholic education. In a world of increasingly rapid change, and greater personal freedom, pluralism will undoubtedly become more widespread, but the attraction of a school devoted to the ideals of Jesus of Nazareth, especially the dialectic, and at times apparently irreconcilable demands of freedom and truth, will continue to lure idealistic teachers of good will and parents anxious to give their children the opportunity to mature in an educational atmosphere nurtured by Gospel values.

Though the main focus of this article has been the future of Catholic voluntary schools, I feel I cannot finish without a brief but sincere acknowledgement of the wonderful way Catholic teachers are bringing the message of Jesus to young people in

State, especially VEC schools throughout the country. Often these teachers are struggling with less academically-gifted children, and with inadequate support, but they are, nevertheless, striving to uphold Gospel values, especially those of welcome, acceptance, kindness and compassion. Would it not be ironic if the teachers in these schools surpassed their colleagues in Catholic second-level schools in their efforts to foster an ethos, which, though perhaps not as overtly Catholic, was, nevertheless, effective in upholding Gospel values!

NOTES

1. D. Leader and S. Boldt, *Principals and Principalship: A Study of Principals in Voluntary Secondary Schools* (Dublin: Marino Institute of Education, 1994), p. 4.
2. Patrick Diggins, 'A Study of the Task of the Principal in Second-Level Schools in Ireland', in G. K. Williams and D. Herron, *Achievement and Aspiration: Curricular Initiatives in Irish Post-Primary Education in the 1980s* (Dublin: Drumcondra Teacher's Centre, 1990), p. 127.
3. Leader and Boldt, op. cit., p. 4.
4. Vatican Congregation for Catholic Education, *The Religious Dimension of Education in a Catholic School* (Dublin: Veritas, 1988), p. 38.
5. Dermot A. Lane, *Catholic Education and the School: Some Theological Reflections* (Dublin: Veritas, 1991), p. 25.
6. *The Religious Dimension of Education in a Catholic School*, op. cit., p. 34.
7. Ibid.
8. Vatican II, *Gravissimum educationis* (Declaration on Christian Education), in Flannery (ed.), *Documents of Vatican II* (Dublin: Dominican Publications, 1981), p. 8.
9. J. J. Alviar, *Klesis: The Theology of Christian Vocation According to Origen* (Dublin: Four Courts Press, 1993).
10. Ibid.
11. E. Fuller (ed.), *The Christian Idea of Education* (Oxford: Oxford University Press, 1957).
12. Ibid.

13. Ibid., pp. 228-30.
14. F. H. Hilliard, *Hibbert Lectures 1965* (London: Allen & Unwin, 1965), pp. 19-20.
15. Ibid.
16. Gabriel Moran, *Design for Religion: Towards Ecumenical Education* (New York: Herder and Herder, 1970).
17. *The Tablet,* 17 December 1994, p. 1623.
18. *The Tablet,* 19 November 1994, p. 1488.
19. *The Tablet,* 26 November 1994, p. 1526.
20. *The Tablet,* 17 December 1994, p. 1623.
21. *The Religious Dimension of Education in a Catholic School,* op. cit., p. 6.
22. Ibid., p. 26.
23. 1982, p. 1.

THE FAMILY AS A SYSTEM

Liam Ryan

It has become a cliché to say that we live in a time of change. This is particularly true of Ireland where the process of change and of modernisation has been telescoped into a much shorter time span than elsewhere. Changes that took a century and a half in other western countries are taking place in Ireland in the space of a single generation. Our current debates on family legislation, divorce, contraception and abortion, are a good example of this. In Britain, the main debate on divorce took place in the mid-nineteenth century, that on contraception in the early decades of this century, and that on abortion in the 1930s and again in the 1960s. In Ireland these issues are debated not just in the same year or month but on the same television programme. Not just in family matters but in all areas of social change, Ireland is today an intriguing laboratory where one can study in a condensed form the trends and changes found in other countries over a much longer term.

Nostalgia for a time when life was simpler is a common response to disturbing changes in family life as in social life generally. People often find it comforting to think of a time when family values were strong and when the value of family living was held in high esteem. This nostalgic feeling is by no means confined to Ireland. In the field of academic sociology, it has often been said that the decade of the 1950s was the 'golden age' of the so-called nuclear family. Due to the influence of American sociologist Talcott Parsons, what might be called the standard sociological theory of the family was then established and continued to have a deep and lasting effect which extended far outside the United States.

Functionalist theory

One of the most influential versions of standard sociological theory was structural functionalism. According to this approach, any major social institution such as the family must meet the needs of its members for personal development and also the needs of the society upon which these individuals depend. The family was seen to be an adaptive unit which mediates between the individual and society. It performs 'functional prerequisites', or essential functions, for its members and for society. Consequently, the smooth functioning of family life must be vital for the well-being of any society. More importantly, it follows that in a normally functioning society, when the needs and structure of the larger society change the forms of family life will also change to ensure that society's needs continue to be met. Parsons claimed that in modern western societies the family has adapted to meet the demands of an industrial economy. He argued that industrialisation brought with it the 'conjugal family' (because it is founded on marriage) or what he more usually called the 'nuclear family' (because it is a minimal social group of father, mother, children).[1] Along with other functionalists he argued that this type of family is the only type that does not conflict with the requirements of a modern industrial society. It facilitated, since it was small, greater labour mobility; it left the husband free from kinship pressures at work; the mother played a key emotional role in the home; and the independent nuclear family household provided emotional support for parents and children in a highly competitive and impersonal society.

The systems approach
The functionalist approach, which was just one of many possible ways of studying the family, emphasised the family as a social system and as one of the many components of the complete social system (society). Characteristically, studies employing this approach view the family both as an internal system for regulating relations within the family and as an external system for dealing with the transactions between the family and non-family agencies and events. The framework thus includes (1) the relationship between the family and systems like the school, the occupational world, the market place and the State, and (2) the transactions between the family as a whole and the smaller subgroups of husband and wife, cliques among the children, and the individual personality systems of family members.

Internally, the family itself is composed of individuals who are best studied through their status and roles and who are significant for their functions in the maintenance of the family system. In this sense the family is seen as a system which tends to maintain its boundaries or, in plain language, its privacy. Individuals contribute to the boundary maintenance of the system either by acting in response to the demands of their structure or by acting under the constraints of the structure, i.e. by 'closing ranks' either willingly or unwillingly. The family structure generally includes the expectations of other members that boundary maintenance will be preserved. We shall see later that this can be counter-productive where family members maintain their silence on child abuse, physical violence and wife battering.

The family as a whole, then, is best studied for the functions it performs for society. The term function usually refers to:

1. the part played by a particular unit in the maintenance of the system, or
2. to the interrelationship of the parts that compose the system, or
3. to the relationship between the family as a system and the total social system (society).

Before moving on to look at a practical illustration of all this in the modern Irish family, it may be useful to summarise in the words of Reuben Hill who has had a major influence on the sociology of the family in America. According to Hill,[2] the family is a social system because it has the following characteristics:

1. family members are interdependent on one another, in that a change in the behaviour of one member leads to a change in the behaviour of other members;
2. the family is a relatively closed, boundary-maintaining unit
3. the family maintains its equilibrium by adapting to other systems and to society itself;
4. the family is a task-performing unit that copes with the requirements of external agencies in society and with the demands of its members.

Hill expands on the task-performing role of the family by identifying six functions which it performs for its members:

1. physical support through the provision of food, shelter and clothing;
2. addition of new members through reproduction;
3. socialisation of children for adult roles;
4. maintenance of order;
5. maintenance of morale and motivation;
6. production of a variety of goods and services.

David Cheal, Professor of Sociology at the University of Winnipeg, recently gave this verdict on one of the benefits of seeing the family in terms of systems theory:

> Perhaps the main achievement of family systems theory has been to provide an intellectual framework for beliefs in family strengths. From a systems perspective families represent potent therapeutic resources. The potential for positive change is therefore thought to be greatly enhanced when family members are involved in plans for intervention. More generally, systems theories reaffirm the strength of family ties in atomistic modern societies, in which the breakdown of family life is always a possibility. As well, they confirm the resilience of families as groups that are able to gain some control over the conditions of their existence, despite the often disruptive effects of economic, political and military institutions.[3]

Cheal goes on to state that implicit in his optimistic judgement are three ideas about families that are basic to all systems theories and related approaches. These concepts are: family controls, family boundaries and family development. We shall examine each of these in turn after we have located the family as a subsystem more firmly in the wider system of modern Irish society.

Tradition and modernity
It would be a mistake to assume that changes in the family system in Ireland can be neatly summarised as a unilinear transition from a clearly defined starting-point of a traditional family-type to an equally accepted arrival-point of a modern family-type.

The dogged obstinacy of the Irish character, together with the historical fact that each nation fashions its own distinctive version of modernity, should warn us that any simplistic opposition between traditional and modern will scarcely do justice to the complexity of Irish family life. Ireland is today a peculiar mixture of the conservative and the liberal, of the traditional and the progressive, of the religious and the secular, of the dogmatic and the pluralist, all lying uneasily side by side in marvellous complex contradiction. We may be modern enough to want contraception, divorce and maybe abortion but we are traditional enough to want Fianna Fáil rather than the Progressive Democrats to give them to us. Irish Catholics have the highest levels of religious belief and practice in Europe, yet this has apparently proved no obstacle to the widespread practice of contraception or of sexual activity before marriage. Over 20 per cent of all pregnancies in Ireland now occur outside marriage. In 1991, 16.6 per cent of births were non-marital compared to 1.6 per cent in 1961. If we look at first births to mothers, in 1991 32.5 per cent were outside marriage.

Sources of changes

Change has come from two sources: from without due to the disruptive effects of industrial capitalist society, and from within due to the impact of developments in biological and medical research on the future of the family. It may well be that discoveries in human biology are potentially more significant for family life than are technological developments. In addition, the ideological invasion of rationalism, secularism and, more recently, feminism, has had an enormous impact on the family. From the feminist perspective, the proper focus of family studies should not be on any supposed 'crisis' in the modern family or on any evolution from traditional to modern forms of family life but, rather, on the subordination of women in all types of marriages, past and present, worldwide. As a consequence, the concept of family has broadened to include unions based on cohabitation, one-parent families, homosexual and lesbian unions. There are many different kinds of families, not least as a result of the threefold increase in divorce in Britain and America, for instance, since 1970. In

Britain the number of lone-parent families had doubled to over one million since 1970, while the number of 'blended' families has also greatly increased, with one-third of all marriages now involving a remarriage of one partner. The standard nuclear family of father, mother and children now constitutes only 25 per cent of all households in Britain; in Ireland it constitutes 44 per cent, but surprisingly, less than half of all households. More significantly, in Ireland, there are 81,000 households (8.5 per cent) consisting of lone parents and children, with an additional 2 per cent classified as lone parent with children and others, in all over 100,000 households.

Factors shaping the Irish family system

Three factors have been crucial in fashioning the dominant family type in Ireland in the one hundred years after the Famine: firstly, the strength and influence of Irish Catholicism; secondly, the family-based character of the economy up to the 1960s; and, thirdly, the informal alliance between Church and State which supported traditional family patterns from Independence to the 1970s. The influence of all three factors is now greatly diminished, especially the economic support for traditional family structures.

The acceptance by the vast majority of the population of standard Christian beliefs and practices inevitably promoted equally orthodox beliefs concerning marriage and the family. Such beliefs included an acceptance of lifelong monogamy, chastity before marriage and faithfulness to one's spouse after it, the importance of children, the necessity of a religious ethos in the home and in the school, and the acceptance of guidance from the Church in all matters religious, moral and even social. Today, however, the monolithic orthodox mould has been broken. Ireland has an increasing number of people who see themselves as Catholics, who wish to remain within the Church, but who question the Church's authority over their private lives especially in the area of sexuality, marriage and divorce. Beliefs, values and expectations on all aspects of sexuality and family life appear in Ireland to be moving closer to the European norm but values and attitudes are very unpredictable entities and, indeed, are often a poor predictor of actual behaviour, so that we can expect that Ireland will retain its own distinctive features of marriage and the family well into the twenty-first century.

The shift in Ireland from basing one's life chances on family property to basing them on educational credentials has had a profound effect on many features of the Irish family. In the 1920s, over half of all young men who remained in Ireland were engaged in family employment that would eventually give them inheritance of the family farm or business and family home. By the end of the century, this is true of only 15 per cent of any agegroup. In 1926, for instance, 55 per cent of the entire male labour force was engaged in family employment. With both employment and prospective property-owning largely determined by family inheritance, this concentrated enormous power in the hands of the father. It created an authoritarian family pattern which persisted in Ireland much later than in the rest of Europe and which gave to Irish marriages more of an economic than a biological function.

The economic base of the majority of Irish families no longer lies in small-scale family enterprises, whether farms or small businesses. The shift from property to wages and salaries as the basis of income has, on the one hand, given children an economic freedom unknown to previous generations but, on the other, has made them dependent on parents for a much longer period while they acquire the educational credentials necessary to compete in the market-place. It is scarcely surprising that married women demand the same freedoms and are no longer satisfied to be economically dependent on men. The main impact of industrialisation on the family has been to make children, and increasingly wives, dependent on the labour market, or on the State in the case of the unemployed, rather than on fathers or husbands for a livelihood. In the process, the family has ceased to be largely father-centred. The traditional Irish family gave the father a powerful means of authority over his children and wife. It was a system in which children contributed to the family home much more than they ever received in return. In the modern family, with children dependent on parents often till their early twenties, the pattern is reversed. In material terms parents give to children much more than they ever receive in return. The result is to greatly increase the cost of children to parents, leading in turn to one of the more universal features of the modern family, the dramatic decline in family size.

The gradual growing apart of Church and State in Ireland since the 1960s has been largely amicably achieved on the basis of consensus rather than conflict. In the process, the Catholic Church came to define more clearly, especially in the 1970s, the distinctions between the religious and civil role of citizens. In formally acknowledging that the civil law need not always prohibit what was contrary to the moral law, the Church left legislators free to form their own views about the balance of social gain and loss on moral issues. The fact that the Church did not always adhere to this principle in recent decades may partially explain why the Supreme Court rather than Dáil Éireann has been the most important agent of change in family law. From the McGee case of 1973 to the 'X' case of 1992, the Supreme Court has been active in expanding individual rights, in redefining women's rights and in interpreting the Constitution in a broadly liberal manner, all of which have had far-reaching implications for laws governing sexuality, marriage and the family. Significantly, in responding to the Court's ruling in the 'X' case, the Irish Hierarchy and the electorate took a major step in a liberal direction in the subsequent three-part referendum on abortion. Given the unpredictability and, at times, the sheer perversity of the Irish character, it would be a foolhardy individual, indeed, who would predict that this liberal swing will continue either in the Supreme Court or in the hierarchy or in the electorate.

Adaptation of the family system to social change
On the basis of these trends in family life we can summarise the manner in which the family as a system adapts to the wider changes in the social system as a whole. It may be appropriate to think of these changes in terms of a three-stage developmental model.

A. *The pre-industrial household*
The first stage is the pre-industrial household economy of which the traditional Irish farm family is a good example. Here the family is a work unit as well as a residential unit with tasks segregat-

ed by age and sex, with the husband controlling income and decision-making and the wife's duties extending well beyond the domestic tasks associated with modern housework. The survival of this traditional family type in Ireland, sometimes called the stem-family system, attracted considerable scholarly interest in the first half of this century. Social scientists like the Harvard anthropologists Arensberg and Kimball were able to study in Ireland a family system that had earlier been the norm over much of western Europe. They explicitly stated that 'the Irish small farmers behave as they do because they are members of a social system of a certain kind; a system implies a state of equilibrium in which elements are in mutual dependence; if change is introduced at one point, change follows at another.'[4]

The authors go on to analyse the family system in terms of three cycles of change: the daily round which makes up the work of women – this revolves around the farmhouse; the yearly round which defines the work of men – this revolves around the farm; and, finally, encompassing all members of the family, the life cycle – birth, first communion, marriage, retirement, and death. In many ways, their study is an example of the subordination of individual needs of family members to those of kinship and the social system. It tries to show that however traditional and antiquated family practices in rural Ireland of the 1930s might seem by more modern standards, these characteristics made sense and 'functioned' in their own terms, and formed a logical, distinctive, cohesive system different from that of the industrialised world.

B. *The industrial household*

We have already seen how a new type of family emerged in response to the needs of the new industrial order. This new type was regarded by Parsons as highly 'functional': its small size, consisting only of a married couple and their children, facilitated the kind of mobility required by the new industrial cities and rapidly changing labour needs; it was relatively independent of kin and community and so could relocate quickly if necessary; and as this new nuclear family was viewed more as a passively adapting element of the system than as an agent of change, it could readily respond to the requirements of the total system.

This was, above all else, the family system adapted to the arrival of salaried and wage labour as the dominant source of income. Here the bread-winner husband goes off to work while the stay-at-home housewife concentrates on household and childcare within the home. There emerges a clear polarisation between the non-household wage sector dominated by men and the unpaid household sector which is seen as the woman's preserve. In Ireland, this restriction of married women to domestic roles was intensified by the setting up of formal legal prohibitions on the employment of married women outside the home. As the family lost some of its functions, leaving education to the schools, work to the office and factory, health to the State, and the care of the old to institutions, it was seen to be freed to concentrate on providing human warmth and intimacy in an increasingly impersonal larger society. The expectation that married couples would establish their own independent households helped to emphasise this 'expressive function' of the modern nuclear family.

C. *The post-industrial household*

The third stage in the developmental model of the family is marked by the large-scale entry of married women into the labour force as service employment takes over from manufacturing employment as the main source of jobs. An essential element in the emergence of this stage is the decline in the number of children per family to the point that housework becomes a very small part of a family's concern or is equally shared by husband and wife.

Two very striking trends in family life are evident throughout the western world, that towards smaller families and that towards greater participation by wives in the labour force outside the home. These trends are clearly interrelated. The value of the work which a wife does in the home is obviously related to the number of children she has to care for. On the other hand, a wife's education, training and experience in the work-force are key factors in assessing the amount of income foregone as a result of leaving her job to care for home and children. With the rise in women's educational standards, the increase in job opportunities open to them, and the reduction in the amount of housework, the reason why a woman should give up a job or a career is closely related to the number of children she chooses to have. The result has been a marked reduction in the number of children per family.

Continental European countries have been much more concerned with family policy, in the formal official sense, than have countries like Ireland, Britain or the United States. Family policy in Europe has and continues to be a form of population policy. In the early part of the present century fears of population decline, as evidenced by falling birth rates, featured prominently among the concerns of governments in France, Germany and Sweden, anxious as they were about their military and economic prospects *vis-à-vis* one another. One of the most striking and dramatic changes in fertility rates in Europe is the sudden drop in birth rates all across the Mediterranean world in the past four years. The birth rates in Italy, Spain, Portugal and Greece are now well below the northern European average. Italy has, in fact, at nine births per thousand population, the lowest birth-rate in Europe. While the decline in Ireland has been also dramatic, it remains, at fourteen per thousand population, higher than the northern European average and well ahead of the Mediterranean level. The number of births in Ireland has dropped from a peak of 74,000 in 1980 to something over 51,000 today.

While most western countries are dominated by third-stage household types, Irish households still retain some vestiges of the first stage, have moved largely to the second stage, and show some signs of evolution to the third stage. Unpaid work in the home is still the principal occupation of over 60 per cent of Irish women. If we leave aside the four-year olds and under, the Irish population today roughly divides into one million in paid employment, one million at school and one million neither at work or in school. With little prospect of that pattern changing over the next decade, the progression to the third-stage family type may be still somewhat far off.

Internal adaptation of the family system

According to David Cheal, 'a system is a set of interacting elements (the 'parts' of the system), which is capable of maintaining a 'boundary' between itself and the outside world, and which enters into transactions (or 'exchanges') with its environment'.[5]

Nowadays, a multiplicity of agencies works with families for a variety of purposes – welfare systems, health systems, educational systems, churches, courts, social workers and family therapists in increasing numbers. This is, to some extent, the public face of the family. But the concept of a social system also assumes that families as systems must possess a private dimension, a degree of separation from their surroundings. How has this private aspect of the modern family adapted to its new internal environment?

We have already seen that this adaptation can best be understood in terms of three concepts: family controls, family boundaries and family development.

A. *Family controls*

The dominant functionalist perspective of Talcott Parsons, despite its emphasis on the idea of system, had analysed society, including the family, largely in terms of structural concepts – norms, roles, statuses, institutions, authority. Over-concentration on these made for a rather static, if not mechanical, view of society. From the early 1970s onwards, Parsons' views came to be supplemented by what was called 'modern systems theory', a focus on living systems which, no matter what the environment, appeared to have the capacity for growth and development. In contrast, the systems in Parsons' horizon moved only towards equilibrium, decay and death.

A key concept in modern systems theory, which originated in engineering, was the capacity of a system to control its own behaviour through 'feedback'. The concept of 'feedback' refers to the way in which a system can monitor its own behaviour and can feed this information into a decision-making process. Feedback is a built-in evaluating mechanism which reacts to the behaviour of the system and incorporates into it the consequences of its own behaviour. As a result, the system's behaviour is changed.

In the traditional Irish family control was achieved largely through lack of feedback and the absence of communication. An authoritarian father controlled not merely the money and resources of the system but also the major decisions the future of the system's members. This traditional family provided a good system in which to bring up children, but only to the age of fifteen or thereabouts. After that there was silence in the home, silence in the school, and silence in the community about the children's future. The dominant father often remained silent even on the question of which of the children might inherit his property.

A second concept in modern systems theory is the distinction between closed and open systems. The traditional Irish family was more often than not a closed system with roles and statuses clearly defined and lines of demarcation between men's, women's and children's work seldom breached. Arensberg and Kimball concentrate especially on this aspect of family life in Co. Clare in the 1930s. Today, the model of the family is more that of an open system, continually adjusting and redirecting itself on the basis of 'feedback', information and discussion. It is a much more democratic system. Hannan and Katsiouni's 1977 study of families in the west of Ireland found that the traditional autocratic family then constituted only 10 per cent of families and, not surprisingly, that it had the highest rate of wife dissatisfaction. Classifying families on the basis of segregated work roles, decision-making, and social-emotional roles, the researchers found a plurality of farm family types. What they describe as 'modern with husband leadership' was the most common type at 25 per cent and with one of the highest levels of wife satisfaction with her husband's role in the family.

B. *Family boundaries*
The 'boundary' is that region separating one system from another. Families as systems possess a degree of separation from their surroundings. That dividing-line is seen as a boundary between what is in the system and what is outside it. Its function is to filter or select the inputs and outputs of the system. This process of selection of what enters and exits the system is governed by the norms of the system. Indeed, in any system or organisation the strictest norms are generally those concerned with boundary maintenance – 'keeping it in the family'.

As already seen, systems can be open or closed. Systems that are highly selective in admitting information from and contributing information to the environment are described as closed. Systems that are less selective are defined as open. Extremely open and extremely closed family systems are both likely to generate problems and are associated with unhealthy forms of family life.

A family in which children are sexually abused or in which a husband's violence results in wife-beating and child-battering is almost always a closed system. There is an overly rigid boundary between the family and the outside world. An explicit rule develops that there 'be no tales out of school' and that family problems be dealt with totally within the family boundary. Women and children maintain the family system, often at great cost to themselves. Indeed they are sometimes thought to reinforce violent behaviour when their silence and compliance provides positive feedback to the abusive husband. The overly rigid boundary maintenance also insulates family members from social feedback from neighbours and teachers, or from professionals like doctors, police or social workers, which might have exerted a corrective influence on closed family behaviour. The lack of negative feedback from those outside the family system is a feature of such closed systems.

Extremely open family systems also have many potential problems. These arise when it becomes difficult to define what or where the family boundaries are or to decide who is and who is not part of the system. The increased incidence of marital breakdown, the increase in non-marital births and the growing pattern of cohabitation can lead to what is called 'boundary ambiguity', sometimes associated with disorganisation in family life. These problems are further aggravated by the increase in the number of 'reconstituted' or 'blended' families now being created as a result of remarriage after divorce. These give rise to new family types which are neither extended families nor nuclear families, and whose members are often uncertain who is in or outside the system.

C. *Family development*
The concept of family development is based on the concept of

the family life cycle of birth, growth and decay. This small, intimate group has a predictable natural history designated by stages, beginning with the husband-wife pair and becoming more complex with the arrival of each additional member, then becoming less complicated as children are launched into jobs and marriages and the group contracts to husband-wife again. At some stages of development parents and children are good company, at other stages their diverse needs and strivings can be quite incompatible.

Family development theory was linked to systems theory from an early point in its evolution. It has been used by family therapists and others dealing with family problems who view stress as being greatest at transition points from one stage to another in the family life cycle. It emphasises the changing internal structure and development of the family and the many concepts associated with the family as a system of interacting actors.

Within the family system there have always been three basic transitions in the lives of young people: from home to school; from school to work; and from the parental home to a home and family of their own. In Ireland today all three transitions take place in a rapidly changing and increasingly insecure social situation. The transition from home to school has occurred in the context of a rapidly expanding youth population and an explosion in the numbers of children now enrolled in Irish schools – close to one million in all. Some 25 per cent leave the educational system with minimal or no qualifications and for them the path to the remaining two transitions is very bleak. At whatever age and with whatever qualifications one leaves, the easy transition from school to work is a thing of the past. A guillotine has fallen and chopped out an empty chunk of time for most youngsters: several years go by before their first job, several years of further dependence on parents and family. The final transition, from the parental home, is necessarily postponed for many young people by the obstacles of unemployment and the insecurity of the job market. This situation is reflected in the drop of 20 per cent in the annual number of marriages in Ireland in the decade of the 1980s, from a total of 21,790 in 1980 to 17,500 in 1990.

Parallel to the drop in the number of marriages is the dramatic increase in the percentage of births outside of marriage.

When one in three of all first time births is non-marital, some dramatic change has surely taken place in the pattern of family life and values in Ireland. While the increase in non-marital births is due to some extent to increasing patterns of cohabitation and second unions after separation, it is also related to unemployment and the achievement of adult status. For many teenaged girls living in a poor family where no one may have worked for years, and with no hope of success in school or in a job, life prospects can be particularly grim. If one cannot become an adult by earning a living and moving from the family home, one can at least achieve some independence, some income and perhaps some status by having a baby. It is not that a girl rationally and calculatingly wants to get pregnant. Rather it is that she has no great incentive to prevent pregnancy. Indeed, in such a depriving world, pregnancy is, in any case, traditionally a preliminary to getting married. Pregnancy may not be planned but, once it happens, it is often no longer unwanted. It is, unfortunately, for some girls, the only alternative path to achieving independence and adult status.

Conclusion

Viewing the family as a system is just one approach among a great many conceptual frameworks used to study the modern family. Each approach has its merits and limitations, and the task of the student of the family is to test the usefulness of these approaches for understanding the complexities of family behaviour.

The main supporters of the systems approach have been those who have built on the standard sociological theory of the mid-twentieth century and who believed that there is a universal entity called the family which performed essential functions for its members and for society.

The major criticism of this approach has come from within the feminist movement. The main complaint was that the sociologists had totally neglected any issues and theories that did not fit the image of the family favoured in standard sociological theory. More particularly, feminists accused the systems approach of too often seeing the family as a unified interest group and ignoring the oppression and conflict endemic in family life. Women's oppression in marriage became the main focus of attention and especially the manner in which this is produced through the collusion of men against women in a variety of institutions.

It is argued that any analysis which sees the family as a system inevitably emphasises the development of the system as a whole while overlooking the subjective concerns of individual members, especially wives and children. According to the feminist perspective, the systems approach offers hidden support for a form of patriarchy, or domination of women by men, in that it takes for granted the individual members' commitment to the existence and continuation of the system. In a family system where continued participation brings few immediate rewards to wives, this commitment may be open to question.

NOTES

1. Talcott Parsons, 'The American Family', in *Socialization and Interaction Process,* T. Parsons and R. Bales (Glencoe: Free Press, 1955).
2. Reuben Hill, 'Modern Systems Theory and the Family', in *Social Science Information,* Vol. 10, 1971; 'Social Theory and Family Development', in *The Family Life Cycle in European Societies,* ed. J. Cuisinier (The Hague: Mouton, 1977).
3. David Cheal, *Family and the State of Theory* (London: Harvester Weatsheaf, 1991), p. 67.
4. C. Arensberg and S. Kimball, *1940 Family and Community in Ireland* (Cambridge, Mass: Harvard University Press, 1977), p. 300.
5. Cheal, op. cit., p. 64.
6. D. Hannan and L. Katsiaouni, *Traditional Families? From Culturally Prescribed to Negotiated Roles in Farm Families* (Dublin: Economic and Social Research Institute, 1977).

FROM EDMUND RICE TO THE GREEN PAPER: SOME REFLECTIONS

J.J. Lee

It may seem a long way from the world of Edmund Rice to that of the Green Paper, *Education for a Changing World,* published in 1992. Yet it may be possible to illuminate some issues of enduring importance by comparing certain aspects of educational experience then and now.

Ireland was a far, far poorer country before the Great Famine than it is today. But precisely because poverty was so widespread, the sense of deprivation among the poor was much less. When access to even elementary education was the privilege of a minority, there was little concept of drop-outs, little notion that those who failed to complete an elementary school curriculum, much less to reach university, were victims of an unjust system. How to salvage a minority from the squalor of normality was the highest objective to which even idealists could realistically aspire. However heroically they laboured, their resources could never stretch to providing mass education.

This had its advantages, however, from a teaching point of view. Precisely because the opportunity of attending Christian Brothers' schools was deemed such a privilege by parents devoted to the welfare of their children, the commitment of the parents, and of many of the children, was much greater than is the case with some of the poorest children today. Although their material resources were limited, teachers at that time did not have to contend with the diversions of a more affluent society, nor adjust to the challenge of teaching in a television age, when the range of interests of children, to say nothing of their concentration spans, are heavily influenced by their exposure to the visual media. If poverty posed serious problems for educators in both periods, the nature of those problems differed considerably.

The early Brothers, whether Christian or Presentation, however ardent their inspiration, however exemplary their dedication, could rescue only a small proportion of children from the ravages of poverty. Even then, they drew their pupils not from the very poorest, who were largely beyond social redemption, but from among those a bit further up, if not much further up, the social ladder. The communities from which their pupils came were poor. But they were not ghettos of poverty. They were representative rather than exceptional. The children did not generally come from 'problem' families. They came, for the most part, from those families whose parents most prized the opportunity of education for their children. Home-school liaison required a far less elaborate structure than that imposed by the culture of poverty today, where so many problem children reflect problem parents, or at least parents trapped in a culture of poverty.

The Green Paper rightly recognises the baneful consequences for children of impoverished home backgrounds. But it still expects too much from the school and the teacher. Schools cannot and should not be expected to compensate for the problems arising from structural poverty in our society. Ireland is not today a poor country by international standards. Yet poverty in Ireland is not primarily a consequence of the personal inadequacy of the poor. That is inevitably the case for some, but I know of no evidence to suggest that it is the case with the vast majority. It arises, for the most part, from the way we chose to structure our society. We have chosen to create poverty in the midst of relative plenty. We have accepted, even contributed to, the emergence of a culture of poverty in a number of specific areas – in inner-city Dublin, in a circle of suburbs on the west side of Dublin, in parts of the northside of Cork, and in South Hill in Limerick. Of course poor individuals, or poor families, can be found everywhere, in rural as well as in urban areas. But the culture of poverty, by which I mean lifestyles and casts of mind that are habituated by unemployment or low wages to think in terms of life without work or without incentive, who seek escape from the hopelessness of their work situation by sinking into a dependency syndrome, drugged into apathy, whether literally by succumbing to a drink or drug culture, or metaphorically by dependence on welfare, flourishes in an urban environment.

The schools cannot, on their own, compensate for the consequences of this culture. Teachers cannot become substitute social workers. Children from these backgrounds are more likely to bring their home culture into the schools than to bring the school culture back home. The home liaison service requires, and deserves, a massive injection of resources in these high priority areas.

It is not possible for teachers today to replicate the earlier social impact of the Christian Brothers. The Brothers moved mountains. But they were generally working with the parental grain, and not, as is often the case with poorer children today, against it.

The success of the Brothers in moulding their often unpromising raw material into coherent shape owed a good deal to their ability to forge a sense of identity among their pupils. They worked hard at establishing their particular ethos. Edmund Rice was determined to inculcate the Catholic faith effectively in his pupils. The main threat to Catholicism in his day came from Protestantism. It is easy today to forget the intensity of the religious conflict, or indeed the superiority of material resources at the disposal of the Protestant Churches in early nineteenth-century Ireland. There was a battle to be fought, and the Brothers were in the front line in defending and promulgating the values of their faith.

The question of values remains central to education. Today, however, the main conflict lies not between Catholic and Protestants, but between religion and irreligion. Secularists like to imagine themselves as beacons of tolerance in contrast to the intolerance they associate with religion in general and with the Catholic Church in particular. Some secularists do strive to foster a genuine sense of tolerance. But they do not predominate among their kind. By tolerance, some seem to mean indifference. Others have no difficulty reconciling their rhetorical commitment to tolerance with a rabid anti-Catholicism. Their tolerance ends where Catholic values begin. It was instructive, for instance, to observe the reticence of secularists in the media when Archbishop Eames of Armagh made a robust defence of the right of Protestants to preserve the ethos of their schools. He was entitled to do so, and in my view right to do so. Had the Catholic

Primate championed the Catholic ethos in equally vigorous terms, however, it seems safe to surmise he would have been roundly condemned by secularist propagandists.

It is becoming increasingly clear that the basic conflict in Ireland, as throughout the world, is between the spiritual and the material, however variable the guise in which the spiritual expresses itself in different cultures. The Northern tragedy has tended to disguise the fact that in Ireland Catholic and Protestants have essentially far more in common with one another than either has with materialist ideologies. Conflict between them increasingly smacks of civil war within the religious community. In that sense, Irish society has changed greatly since the time of Edmund Rice.

The Green Paper sharply criticises the inherited exam system which 'is strongly biased towards acquiring factual knowledge, rather than developing critical thinking and problem-solving skills'. The Brothers have been historically closely associated with the inculcation of factual knowledge as the basis of good education. They were not unique in that. They simply practised more effectively than most what many other teachers, whether religious or lay, Catholic or Protestants, Irish, English, or German, themselves preached and practised in the nineteenth and for much of the twentieth century.

Many educators have reacted against what they saw as an excessive emphasis on 'mere memory', and on rote learning, and have sought to promote more child-centred educational practices. That is highly desirable in itself. It has only become possible in recent decades as the resources devoted to education have increased. A child-centred curriculum would simply have been impossible in nineteenth century circumstances, where class sizes, teacher availability, reading material, etc. precluded the possibility.

But it may be asked if the pendulum has not now swung too far in the opposite direction. For some educationalists, 'critical thinking' and 'problem-solving skills' have come to be seen as an alternative to 'factual knowledge'. But the assumption that critical thinking can be developed without factual knowledge of the subject to which one applies one's critical thinking simply flies in the face of experience in the real world. 'Factual knowledge' does not guarantee a capacity for critical thought. But it is virtually impossible to achieve critical thought, at least about society, without factual knowledge. Ignorance does not guarantee intelligence.

The sharp distinction drawn between 'factual knowledge' and 'critical thinking' or 'problem-solving skills' may also overlook the fact that the acquisition of factual knowledge may remain the most effective way of inculcating those qualities of concentration and discipline, which are not only valuable in themselves, but also contribute significantly towards a capacity for critical thinking and problem-solving. It may be that genius can rely on flashes of cosmic inspiration to penetrate the mysteries of their subjects. But most of us rely on more mundane and protracted processes of diagnosis and prescription. It may even be argued that in a televisual world of primarily materialistic impulses, where the clamour for the 'instant fix' has become so dominant a popular impulse, that it is precisely those qualities of application and concentration that are most urgently needed, not only at school, but in the wider society. The tendency in the Green Paper to view the two approaches as mutually exclusive rather than as mutually supportive is distinctly unfortunate.

Two other themes which feature prominently in the Green Paper as essential objectives of educational reform, the creation of 'an enterprise culture' and education 'for citizenship of Europe' raise interesting issues in the context of Edmund Rice's perspective on education.

Rice was himself a successful businessman before he entered his religious vocation. As the founder of the Christian and Presentation Brothers, he was an outstanding exponent of enterprise in the wider sense of the term, a risk-taker of extraordinary vision and courage. But his motivation in this work was not the maximisation of private profit, now extolled as the supreme human value. If 'enterprise culture' is simply a euphemism for worship at the altar of greed, it could have no place in the value system of Edmund Rice.

At a more mundane level, however, the Christian and Presentation Brothers traditionally educated pupils for work as well as for life. Edmund Rice himself took care to place the pupils who came through his schools in employment. Parents did not send their children to the Brothers to prepare them for a life of leisure and ease. They couldn't afford to. Their children had to earn their living. The qualities of determination, order and reliability which a Christian/Presentation Brothers education helped inculcate in most of their pupils themselves contributed to potential economic development if other circumstances happened to be propitious. Why those circumstances were often not propitious in Ireland raises far wider questions than the relation of education to 'an enterprise culture'.

The insinuation that 'an enterprise culture' requires the rejection of a whole inherited teaching tradition seems to me unsustainable. What is undoubtedly true is that the world of work has itself changed dramatically in recent decades, and that the traditional teaching techniques of the Brothers, as of many other institutions – not excluding universities – took some time to adapt, in so far as adaptation may be deemed desirable. It remains legitimate, as it always has been, to ask of every level of education how it prepares its charges for both the world of work and the wider life outside. But that is a very big question, raising issues that cannot be answered solely on the basis of technocratic criteria.

The Green Paper enthusiastically espouses the preparation of pupils for 'citizenship of Europe'. There is nothing in the philosophy of Edmund Rice inimical to this ideal. Indeed, he might well have had a deeper appreciation of the meaning of 'citizenship of Europe' than many who deem themselves nowadays to be 'Europeans'. 'Europe' for many Irish simply means subsidies from Brussels. After twenty years membership of what is now the European Union, can we really claim that we have a deeper appreciation of European culture, a greater understanding of European history, more affinity with a European identity, than we had before our entry to the EEC? It is desirable that we should learn more European languages in order to be able to sell more products in European markets. From the point of view of European identity, however, it is even more important that we should learn more European languages in order to grasp the essence of the great cultures of Europe. Otherwise Europe simply becomes a geographical expression.

Edmund Rice was deeply concerned with educating citizens for Ireland. Citizenship was an elusive concept in his time, one which hardly penetrated down the social scale to the classes from which the early Brothers drew their pupils. The qualities their education inculcated made for good citizens – citizens of Ireland in the first instance. This itself marked a major step forward for pupils whose horizons rarely stretched beyond the local, and whose concept of civic culture was distinctly limited. The Brothers forged identity among their pupils by building a concept of citizenship around a blend of religion and nationality. They have come in for bitter criticism on this score recently, as if there were something sinister or deviant about this approach. But this was the standard formula in nineteenth-century European education. The Brothers were representative of the main European educational tradition of the time, not deviants from it. That formula could be abused if taken to extremes. But it did focus consciously on the creation of citizens.

The Green Paper seems to take 'citizenship of Ireland' virtually for granted. It does not systematically face the question of how students can be equipped 'more effectively for citizenship of Ireland' in the rapidly changing value systems of today. Where Edmund Rice sought to shape the character of citizenship, the Green Paper seems, on the whole, to be content to follow the future.

One could list, in a fairly mechanical fashion, other features of Edmund Rice's educational system and compare them with those advocated in the Green Paper. But that would be largely unhistorical. Details depend mainly on historical circumstances. It is fundamental values that have to be identified. The biggest difference between the principles of Edmund Rice and the apparently dominant principles of the Green Paper is that there was a hard core of values in Rice's thinking, whereas there seems to be no comparable core of values at the centre of the Green Paper. Maybe this is unfair to the Green Paper. Maybe it took core values so much for granted that it felt able to concentrate on issues of detail. Or maybe not. There are numerous individual recommendations and observations in the Green Paper that, to my way of thinking, are highly laudable. There are several references to the importance of values. Yet one gets the impression that the Green Paper incorporates a variety of viewpoints and that in so far as there is a dominant ethos, it is that of 'enterprise culture', conceived in a peculiarly narrow and myopic sense. Maybe there is little sense of enduring values any more, no vision of the type of society, as distinct from the type of economy, Ireland ought to be. It will be instructive to see how the long-awaited White Paper deals with this fundamental issue.

WHAT OF CHRISTIAN FEMINISM?

Bernadette Flanagan PBVM

Christian feminism is a movement within Christianity that seeks to explore how the fullness of the Gospel, in the area of gender relations, is not yet being lived. It draws attention to distortions that have crept into the Gospel message as it accommodated itself to a patriarchal culture. Since it is predominantly concerned with uncovering the feminine face of the Christian tradition it has been termed 'feminist'. However, it seeks to be true to a Gospel preached so that all would know life to the full (Jn 10:10), and so does not seek simply to reverse patterns of gender oppression. Rather its concern is to work for new relationships between the sexes in the Christian community which could be more life-giving for both, but at the price of change. I will first trace the emergence of this call for a new understanding of the position of women in family, Church and society and the challenges it poses for gender relations. I will then explore how the way we name God can contribute to promoting the new attitudes being called for. Finally, I will look at that ancient story which has been so formative of attitudes between the sexes in family, society and Church; the creation of Adam and Eve.

Catholic social teaching

The call in the Scriptures to 'act justly' is, according to the root meaning of the Hebrew word for 'justice', a call to build right relationships in the community. A body of writings collectively termed Catholic Social Teaching (CST) teases out the implications of this call for the contemporary world. Leo XIII's encyclical *Rerum novarum* (1891) was the first document in a now extensive collection of writings ranging over issues such as workers' rights, international debt and the ecological crisis. In these writings the area of gender relations is also introduced as one of the key areas to which the Christian community needs to give urgent attention. While in the social encyclicals of the Popes from Leo XIII to Pius XII one finds views on gender roles similar to those in the society of their day, a change in perception begins to emerge in the writings of John XXIII. In the encyclical *Pacem in terris* (1963) he reflects on three movements that characterise the present age and to which the Christian community needs to attend. Referring to the second of these movements he notes:

> The part that women are now playing in political life is everywhere evident. This is a development that is perhaps of swifter growth among Christian nations, but it is also happening extensively if more slowly among nations that are heirs to different traditions and imbued with a different culture. Women are gaining an increasing awareness of their natural dignity. Far from being content with a purely passive role or allowing themselves to be regarded as a kind of instrument, they are demanding both in domestic and public life the rights and duties which belong to them as human persons. (n. 41)

While John XXIII sounds a note of approval for the new roles being assumed by women in the public sphere, Paul VI presents the first hints of a changed understanding of the roles of men and women in the family. In the Pastoral Constitution *Gaudium et spes* (1965) he states:

> The family is a kind of school of deeper humanity. But if it is to achieve the full flowering of its life and mission, it needs the kindly communion of minds and the joint deliberation of spouses, as well as the painstaking cooperation of parents in the education of their children. The active presence of the father is highly beneficial to their formation. (n. 52)

In the same paragraph he later adds that the 'domestic role of hers [the mother] must be safely preserved, though the legitimate social progress of women should not be underrated on that account'. The most remarkable aspect of this paragraph is of course the fact that it mentions the necessity of the presence of the father to the children. Unlike earlier papal documents this one also has much less differentiation of the duties of parents by sex. In addition there is an effort to affirm those women called to full-time parenting and those called to other social roles. A later paragraph focuses on the rights of all 'to a human and civic culture favourable to personal dignity and free from any discrimination on the grounds of race, *sex* [emphasis mine], nationality, religions, or social conditions' (n. 60).

The end of the same paragraph returns to the subject of women's changing social role:

> Women are now employed in almost every area of life. It is appropriate that they should be able to assume their full proper role in accordance with their own nature. Everyone should acknowledge and favour the proper and necessary participation of women in cultural life. (n. 60)

Here he is encouraging the changes necessary to remedy the situation he has presented as regrettable:

> It is regretted that basic personal rights are not yet being respected everywhere, as is the case with women who are denied the chance to freely choose a husband, or a state of life, or to have access to the same educational, cultural benefits as are available to men. (n. 29)

Some years later, in 1973, Paul VI established a study commission on the role of women in society and Church in preparation for International Women's Year in 1976. He defined their task as 'concerned with documentation and with reflection on the ways of promoting the dignity and responsibility of women', and he added that 'the fulfilment of the task must be gradual' since 'nothing is gained by talking of the equalisation of rights, for the problem goes far deeper'. Thus the writings of Paul VI open up for discussion the question of the new relation between men and women in family, Church and society. While encouraging this development his own views on the issue are often ambiguous. In some ways he makes more positive statements concerning the similarities of the duties and functions of men and women in society than do his predecessors. And yet, it is true, as Christine Gudorf points out in chapter 5 of her *Catholic Social Teaching on Liberation Themes*, that he uses many of the traditional formulas and views of his predecessors concerning the special nature of women and the appropriate tasks determined by that nature.

The issue of changing gender relations has been a subject of reflection for the current pontiff. In his Apostolic Letter *The Dignity of Women* (*Mulieris dignitatem*) John Paul II reminds us that 'woman remains disadvantaged or discriminated against, by the fact of being a woman' (n. 10). Such a situation contravenes 'the unambiguous content of the evangelical message'. He likens the challenge to remedy the situation of women's disempowerment to the effort necessary to abolish slavery:

> Saint Paul not only wrote: In Christ Jesus.....there is no more man or woman', but also wrote: 'there is no more slave or freeman'. Yet how many generations were needed for such a principle to be realised in the history of humanity through the abolition of slavery! (n. 24)

In the same paragraph he deals also with the issue of evangelical texts which might be construed as presenting a contrary and unequal view of woman's place in home, Church or society. Amongst these he includes:

> Wives submit to your husbands for that is what you should do as Christians. (Col 3:18)

> Train younger women to be good housewives who submit to their husbands. (Tit 2:4-5)

> The husband is supreme over his wife...woman was created for man's sake. (1 Cor 11:3.9)

> In all the churches of God's people the women should keep quiet in the meetings. They are not allowed to speak; as the Jewish law says 'they must not be in charge'. It is a disgraceful thing for a woman to speak in church. (1 Cor 11:33-35)

> I do not allow women to teach or to have authority over men, they must keep quiet... It was not Adam who was deceived, it was the woman who was deceived and broke God's law. (1 Tm 2:11-15)

While the innovation of Christ, as stated by Paul in 'there is no difference between Jews and Gentiles, slaves and free, men and women' (Gal 3:28), is a fact, these writings, John Paul points out, at times reflect more the environment in which they were written than the content of the Gospel.

> The apostolic writings... also express what is 'old': what is rooted in the religious tradition of Israel, in its way of understanding and explaining the sacred texts, as for example the second chapter of the Book of Genesis.

It is clear at this point that John Paul wishes to refute any misuse of the above texts which may have contributed to the subordination of women in familial, social or ecclesial life. Finally, what is evident from this brief review of CST is that the Christian feminist agenda is not simply the concern or responsibility of some discontented women; instead the entire Christian community has been called to find new ways of being men and women of the Gospel together and to make alive the 'innovation of Christ'.

Mother God

> All the evils that have resulted from dignifying one sex and degrading the other may be traced to this one central insight: a belief in a trinity of masculine Gods in One from which the feminine element is wholly eliminated.[1]

Ever since Matilda Joslyn Gage (1826-98) identified the centrality of the gender of God language for the ordering of relationships at all levels in society the issue has been explored from numerous perspectives. Phyllis Trible's writings have highlighted the significant but under-utilised feminine imagery for God in the Hebrew Bible. Elaine Pagels has shown how in early Christianity a great pluralism of symbols for the divine prevailed, and questions why the mother symbol became associated only with Gnostic groups declared heretical by the mainstream Church. Caroline Walker Bynum has unearthed the enormous metaphorical freedom of the mystical tradition, drawing particular attention to the motherhood of God theme developed by such writers as Julian of Norwich, Christina of Markyate, Anselm of Canterbury and Bernard of Clairvaux. Finally, Sallie McFague, in her attempts to remythologise Christian faith through metaphors and models appropriate for an ecological, nuclear age, draws specifically on that strand of the tradition which emphasises the motherhood of God.

That these areas of research are being developed precisely at a time when women are becoming aware of their often unequal position in family, society or Church is not accidental. Rather the insight of Matilda Joslyn Gage is coming to be shared by the larger community. Sandra Schneiders, in her Madeleva lecture (1986), 'Women and the Word: The Gender of God in the New Testament and the Spirituality of Women', has articulated well the three points of intersection between the unequal position of women and the gender of God language. Firstly, she argues that the maleness of Jesus has been used to present maleness as normative for humanity, and men as superior to women. Secondly, she holds that an emphasis on the 'fatherhood' of God has legitimised patriarchy. Thirdly, she believes that the masculinity of God and of Jesus has been used to deny the likeness of woman to God and to Christ.

The proposition that a connection exists between the unequal position assigned to many women in family and society and the gender of God language is not purely speculative. Susan Brooks Thistlethwaite has shown how those whose work brings them into direct contact with women who have experienced family violence often witness to the existence of such links. Sociological research has also shown that amongst the factors that contribute to a cultural configuration which produces a low incidence of rape is an understanding of the sacred as feminine (*Journal of Social Issues*, 37 (1981), 5-27). It is educationally imperative therefore that the rich, but hitherto unfamiliar, Christian tradition of naming God in feminine terms be presented today.

While we commonly think of 'father' as the most common biblical name for God it is interesting to discover that in the entire Hebrew Bible the title is used only fifteen times. In these same writings the images of mother, midwife and wet nurse are also carriers of the people's understanding of their relationship with God. The nurturing concern of God, which the Israelite community captured in the mother image, was amplified in another term, *rahamin*, used to describe Yahweh's love, compassion and mercy. This word is a derivative of the Hebrew for 'womb' and reveals the divine at-homeness in female biology, an insight later lost. Through the image of the midwife the divine is associated with the daring and courageous female spirit. It was the Hebrew midwives, Shiprah and Puah (Ex 1:15-22) who had, after all, enabled the people's liberation from Egypt when they chose to follow their own inner authority, rather than that of the Pharaoh, and allowed Moses to live.

Since all images such as king, mother, shepherd and midwife are partial metaphors, it is necessary to turn to the root metaphor for the divine found in Genesis 1:27 before leaving these writings. There we find:

> And God created humankind in his image;
> in the image of God he created them;
> male and female he created them.

Lines one and two use the common poetic device of inverted parallelism to establish a general resemblance between humanity and the divine. Lines two and three, which lie in straight parallelism, establish that it is male and female together which most fully reflect the divine. Gender relations are thus a privileged revelation of the divine. It is also clear that when considering male and female one is not the fullness of the image of the divine, and the other supplementary or complementary. This is surely a challenge to any familial, social or ecclesial arrangement which claims its ideals from Christianity's normative texts, and yet fails to respect equally the God-image in one sex on grounds of gender.

In contrast to the infrequent use of the term 'father' for God in the Hebrew scriptures, when we turn to the Gospels and other Christian scriptures we find the term being used over one hundred and fifty times. Since, in the earliest Gospel, Mark, Jesus only addresses God as 'father' three times, as compared with over one hundred times in John, the last of the Gospels, scripture scholars believe that there is a demonstrable tendency amongst these early Christian writers to introduce the name 'father' for God into the sayings of Jesus. It is also important to notice that in Jesus' revelation of God he does not avoid the use of feminine imagery. Through the parables of the lost coin and the lost sheep of Luke's Gospel the merciful forgiveness of God is given a feminine and masculine dimension respectively. This Gospel writer also achieves a complementary presentation through the juxtapositioning of God the Baker-woman and God the Sower. Finally, throughout the history of spirituality, those who chose to express their relationship with the divine in female imagery have always found support for their experience in Matthew 23:37, where Jesus presents himself as a mother hen gathering her chicks under her wing.

For the first twelve centuries of Christianity those whose task it was to draw out the meaning of the Christ-event did so primarily by exploring connections and nuances in the Scriptures. Since they came in contact there with female images for the divine we find a comfortable use of these images in their writings. The main features evident in the writers of the time are comparisons of God to a female bird, to the functions of motherhood such as birth and nurturing, and to the fidelity and love of a mother. An extract from Augustine of Hippo's commentary on Psalm 26:10 is representative: 'God is father in that he made, in that he calleth, in that he ordereth, in that he ruleth; mother in that he cherisheth, in that he nourisheth, in that he suckleth, in that he beareth'.

In the twelfth and thirteenth centuries theologians began to experiment with a new way of organising their reflections. Philosophy became the organising science for theology. While this had many advantages in terms of enabling a more systematic exploration of complex issues, it also meant that traditions which were dependent on the Bible for their source, like the female imaging of the divine, were lost. Just as the use of this imagery went into decline in theology, it assumed an unprecedented significance in the language of prayer, as if by psychic compensation. While Anselm of Canterbury initiated devotion to God's motherhood, the seeds sown by him reached their fullest expression in another English writer, Julian of Norwich. She develops her reflection on the motherhood of God in chapters 57 to 63 of her *Showings.* There she asserts that 'the lovely word "mother" is so much its own that it cannot be used properly of any but God'. In contrast to Augustine, however, Julian does not counterbalance motherhood and fatherhood images as if mother was the softer side of a stern, law-giving God. Subsequent to Julian's writings the use of such metaphors went into decline. The stir caused in Italian public opinion when, in an Angelus address, in St Peter's Square in September in 1978, John Paul I invoked God the Mother is evidence of the total disuse into which such metaphors have fallen today. Quoting Isaiah 49:15: 'Can a woman forget her suckling child, that she should have no compassion for the child of her womb?' he said, 'God is a father; more than that, he is a mother'. If Matilda Joslyn Gage's assertion in the introduction to this section is true, then part of the response of educationalists to social systems in crisis must be to retrieve the rich but hidden Christian tradition of inclusive imaging of the divine, for this generation.

Adam and Eve

The sheer frequency with which artists have returned to Genesis 2 and 3 for inspiration for their masterpieces, has ensured that the story of Adam and Eve, rather than the much less detailed creation account of Genesis 1 is the one firmly imprinted on human consciousness. Artistic representations of Eve, taking their cue from theology, have focused on her identity as traitress and temptress. They also captured memorably the connection between woman, sin and Satan by depicting the serpent as female, and even as the mirror-image of Eve. The latter is evident in Lucas Cranach the Elder's (1472-1553) painting *Das Paradies,* which is on display at the Kunsthistorisches Museum, Vienna. In

Michelangelo's *The Temptation* (1511) in the Sistine Chapel an unmistakably female serpent, half woman, half snake, tempts Adam and Eve. Sometimes biblical and mythological traditions were confused and synthesised as in a painting by Jean Cousin (1490-1560) which depicted Eve as the prima Pandora, the one who, like the mythological Pandora, alone bears the responsibility for the evils of the world.

The roots of these artistic representations lie in an intellectual tradition steeped in dualism. This concept posited the existence of a destructive tension between the spirit and the flesh. Rosemary Radford Ruether, in her essay 'Misogynism and Virginal Feminism in the Fathers of the Church', has highlighted how the dualisms of sacred and secular, soul and body, material and spiritual, this world and the next, had emerged in the ancient world prior to Christianity. She then suggests that these polarities became oppressive when they were projected onto the age-old polarity of male and female, with the negatives (secular, body, material, this-worldly) being assigned to women.

It was the logical counterpart of this view that to 'become male' would be a higher state of moral and spiritual perfection for a woman. The fourth-century biblical scholar, Jerome, in a letter to a Spanish benefactor, Lucinius, speaks with esteem of the latter's wife, Theodora, whom he describes as 'once a woman, but now a man'. Shortly after receiving this letter Lucinius died and Jerome, writing to Theodora to console her for her loss, comments how Lucinius' love was evident in that he 'resolved to treat you (Theodora) even on earth as a sister, or indeed I may say, as a brother'.

Finally, the early writings of Christian theology developed an Eve-Mary analogy. In this analogy Mary was presented as the great exception, while Eve was seen as representative of women. The first step along this path was taken by the unknown author of I Timothy, who passed a sharper judgement on Eve than the author of Genesis 3: Adam was not deceived, but the woman was deceived and became a transgressor (I Tim 2:14). It was Tertullian who then proposed that all women share in Eve's sinful character:

And do you not know that you are (each) an Eve? The sentence of God on this sex of yours lives in this age: the guilt must of necessity live too. You are the devil's gateway; you are the unsealer of that (forbidden) tree; you are the first deserter of the divine law; you are she who persuaded him whom the devil was not valiant enough to attack. You destroyed so easily God's image, man. On account of your desert – that is death – even the Son of God had to die.[2]

Given that this understanding of Eve has been received wisdom for almost two millennia we must ask if or how this story ought to be understood today. Firstly, most Scripture scholars hold the view that the creation of woman from the rib of the man signifies their commonality of nature, rather than the secondary nature of the woman. Secondly, the Hebrew word for helper, which is a term used to describe the woman's relationship to the man in Genesis 2:20 can also be translated redeemer or saviour and so does not carry the English connotation of subordinate.

The idyllic scene of chapter 2 gives way to a symbolic representation of the inexplicable fascination of evil in chapter 3. Actively dialoguing with the serpent, and all too easily convinced by him, the woman takes the forbidden fruit and eats. The man accepts the fruit from his partner unquestioningly. Both the active leadership in sin and the passive acquiescence in sin result in equal guilt before God. Lisa Sowle Cahill, in her Madeleva lecture (1992), suggests that the consequent suffering is an ironic reversal:

To the woman, active sinner, God portrays a passive suffering – the pain of childbirth – as well as her husband's 'rule:' over her. To the man, passive sinner who readily but wrongfully consumed the appealing fruit of nature, God portrays an active struggling against the earth.[3]

This judgment of God does not, however, reveal the divine will for humanity's future. Instead, what it shows are the distorting effects of sin on the creation, at a personal, familial and social level. Sexual hierarchy, separation of roles and suffering do not reflect the design of creation but are the manifestation of the presence of sin.

Conclusion

In this essay I have tried to call attention to the call issuing from the social reflections of the teaching Church for a new ordering of relationships between men and women in social, familial and ecclesial structures. These new practices can only take root in a community that is just as much aware of its tradition of imaging God in female terms as it is of its male metaphors for the divine. The birth of this new, but old consciousness will require both the exorcism of the negative history of the Eve symbolism, and the realisation that the closing dialogue between Adam and Eve in the Genesis texts does not reflect the divine design for gender relation in family, Church and society but, rather, indicates the fruits of sin.

NOTES

1. Elizabeth Cady-Stanton *et al* (ed.), *Women, Church and State: History of Woman Suffrage 1* (New York, 1989), pp. 796-97.
2. Tertullian, *The Apparel of Women,* Chapter 1, Section 1, vs. 1-2, in *Fathers of the Church,* Vol. 40, pp. 117-18.
3. Lisa Sowle Cahill, *Madeleva Lecture* (New York: Paulist Press, 1992), p. 28.

SELF-ESTEEM IS THE KEY TO LEARNING

Tony Humphreys

Self-esteem and the school-going child

A child enters a classroom carrying within him or her the effects of relationships with significant adults in his or her life. The most crucial relationship is the one with parents. Children are also affected by their experiences with grandparents (particularly when they live under the same roof), aunts, uncles and child-minders. These relationships are the looking-glass through which the child develops self-esteem. Children, by the time they come to school, have already established an image of themselves, and that image may be further affected by their experiences with teachers and, later on, with peers.

It is now known that children who have learning difficulties in school frequently have self-esteem problems, and that what is needed most before effective academic development can be established is an elevation of their self-esteem. Teachers can do much to raise the self-esteem of children but the involvement of parents is crucial as, most of all, the child needs to be loved and accepted by his or her parents and to impress them. However, if the school-going child has poor self-esteem this means that the parents (biological or foster or adoptive) also have self-esteem difficulties. Parents and teachers with high self-esteem will effect high self-esteem in children but the converse is also true. This process happens whether or not the parents and the other significant adults in the child's life realise it. It is true to say that every action, facial expression, gesture and verbal interaction on the part of significant adults in the child's life communicates some message to the child about his or her worth, value and capability.

The nature of self-esteem

What is self-esteem? There are two central dimensions to self-esteem: the feeling of being lovable and the feeling of being capable. Is your school-going child shy, timid, overly reserved, extremely quiet, attention-seeking and clinging, or aggressive or bullying? If so, these are indications that the child doubts his or her lovability. Is your child frightened of and resistant to new challenges, fearful of failure, easily upset by mistakes, nervous of school tests, perfectionist, overly diligent about school work or evasive of homework? If so, these are indicators of the child's doubts about his or her capability.

Examples of behaviour indicating poor to middle self-esteem are given below. These behaviours are a sign of the inner turmoil of children and positive responses are needed when they are shown. It is useful to categorise these signs as over-control and under-control indicators. Children manifesting under-control of behaviour are more likely to be brought for psychological help. The reason for this is that their problematic behaviours can seriously interfere with parents' and/or teachers' functioning. The child who shows over-control of behaviour is often more at risk but this can be missed by parents and others as the child's symptoms do not upset adults' lives.

Checklist for low self-esteem in school-going children

A. *Over-control indicators:* child may be
   Shy and withdrawn
   Unusually quiet
   Reluctant to take on new activities/challenges
   Clinging to one or both parents
   Having difficulties in mixing with other children
   Overly conscientious or apathetic in learning situations
   Fearful and timid in new situations
   Easily upset when positively corrected
   Extremely upset when negatively corrected
   Inclined to daydream
   Fearful of mistakes and failures
   In the habit of putting him or herself down
   Always trying to please people
   Complaining of abdominal pain and nausea

B. *Under-control indicators:* child may be
   Aggressive
   Having regular temper tantrums

Boastful
Regularly playing truant from school
Uncooperative when requested to do things
Frequently requesting help or reassurance
Continually asking if he or she is loved or wanted
Avoiding school lessons though risking parents' disapproval
Blaming others for his or her mistakes
Destructive of his or her own or others' belongings
Careless when carrying out home or school assignments

Self-esteem and children's learning difficulties

The way parents respond to the self-esteem problems of their children will be determined largely by their own levels of self-esteem. When parents themselves have doubts about their own value and capability they tend to be over-demanding or over-protective or may even be neglectful of their children. Such types of parenting result in the children also having self-esteem difficulties. For example, the children of teachers are more at risk than any other professional group. The reason is that teachers tend to demand high academic performance from their children and tend to scold, ridicule, criticise and condemn failure. All children want to please their parents and the possibility of humiliation through criticism and the withdrawal of love will lead to two possible reactions in children. One reaction is apathy and avoidance. Here the child withdraws from making academic and other efforts because to try means risking humiliation and rejection.

The child sub-consciously reasons: 'with no effort, no failure, no humiliation'. What an immensely clever strategy! But, such children are often labelled 'lazy', 'dull', 'stupid', 'useless'. Without attention to their self-esteem these children will not progress academically.

The second reaction of children when their self-esteem is threatened is compensation. Compensation is evident in the child who is intense or who is a perfectionist, who spends too many hours over schoolwork and who is easily upset by any prospect of failure. Again, the wisdom of the strategy is commendable. By working so hard the child is attempting to eliminate any prospect of failure as failure and mistakes mean risking the disapproval of parents and teachers. This child misses out on other aspects of a child's life such as play, friendship, sports activities and enjoyment of learning. For this child identity is tied to behaviour – particularly academic behaviour – and unless this identity issue is resolved the child will become even more chronically insecure, perfectionist and hard-working as the academic pressures continue to increase during his or her school life-cycle.

There is a second type of compensation which is seen in the child who is boastful, aggressive or bullying and who acts in a superior way. However, he or she rarely makes any effort and any pressure from others to apply himself or herself academically results in a protective response such as: 'I could do it if I wanted to but why should I please you?' Like the child who uses the avoidance strategy or the child who overworks, the child displaying such arrogance is really protecting himself or herself against any possibility of failure, as, once again, failure would mean humiliation and rejection.

Many adults also use these strategies of avoidance and compensation. For example, the most common phobia of all is that of public speaking. Ninety per cent of people avoid such an undertaking. Such avoidance is a clear indicator of people's doubts about their capability and their ability to impress others. Likewise, many parents put high demands and expectations on themselves in order to avoid any prospect of mistake and failure. Many parents say that they have not put verbal pressure on their children to succeed academically. This may be the case, but actions speaks louder than words and it is the parents' lifestyle which mainly affects children. Children believe that their parents are always right and as a result they imitate their actions indiscriminately and become like them. In adolescence children think parents know nothing. But such an attitude is relatively short-lived as the conditioning from childhood is far stronger than this transitory rebellion. Some children will develop a pattern of behaviour that is diametrically opposed to that of their parents. The problem is that this is equally extreme and results in an unhappy and problematic life. For example, the child or adolescent who 'drops out' of school in reaction to pressure for academic performance from parents, builds up a whole new series of problems for himself or herself.

It has been shown that the parent who puts pressure on the child for academic performance, unwittingly damages the child's self-esteem and this leads to either avoidance or compensation by the child to prevent further hurt. But what about the parent who over-protects and puts little or no pressure on children to make responsible efforts? If the overly demanding parent causes children to become insecure and lacking in confidence, the overly protective parent equally brings about similar vulnerabilities in his or her child. The parent, who does everything for the child and does not make reasonable demands of him or her, communicates no message of belief in the child's wondrous capacity to learn and to become independent. Protection disables children and keeps them dependent and helpless. These children may feel loved but they will not feel capable.

Self-esteem and the child's motivation to learn

Many parents are often puzzled by children who clearly possess the skills to learn but make no effort in that direction. The child with high self-esteem retains a natural curiosity for learning and is enthusiastic when presented with a new challenge. This child is confident in social situations and in tackling academic challenges. On the other hand, the child with middle/low self-esteem has lost that excitement of learning; any learning means risking failure and mistakes and these have only brought humiliation and rejection in the past. It is safer to risk a parent's or teacher's disapproval rather than the embarrassment and punishment of failure.

The revealing thing about children is that success and failure in themselves have no effect on their drive to learn, but the reactions of parents, teachers and other significant adults to their success and failure can have a devastating effect on their motivation to learn. When parents (in particular), teachers and others react either positively to successful performance and/or punishingly to failure (e.g. shouting, blaming, scolding, comparing), the child will now begin to doubt his or her ability to live up to expectations. Many parents (and teachers) have difficulty in understanding that praising the successful performance of an activity breeds dependence and fear of failing to please. Parents need to encourage children in their efforts to master an activity. What counts is the effort not the performance. Emphasis on performance may eventually dry up effort, or lead to over-trying. Every effort on a child's part is an achievement.

Think of the child who manages for the first time to put on her shoes: she presents herself to her father and says 'Hey, Dad, look', proudly pointing down at her shoes. Dad looks down and responds crossly 'You put them on the wrong feet'. The child will now feel put down, hurt and rejected. The father has totally failed to understand that this effort is a major achievement: for the first time the child has managed to put her own shoes on her own feet. By showing that he was impressed by her effort, the father could have encouraged and guided the child to learn the next stages of shoe fitting. With the punishing reaction she is unlikely to try again or may get anxious and perfectionist on the next attempt. Without realising it, her father has undermined her self-esteem. This parent has not yet learned that children are always lovable, even if they fail or make mistakes, and that they are immeasurably capable of learning any skill. If the child experiences such punishing parental reactions only now and again, then no serious damage is done to self-esteem. However, if such reactions are a regular feature in a child's life then damage is done to self-esteem.

An important rule for parents to be aware of is that while unrealistic demands lead to low self-esteem, no demands at all lead to low self-esteem (as no confidence is shown in the child's ability). In both cases children are doomed to low academic achievement or over-achievement. The wise parent knows that there is an optimum of pressure – just enough to cause children to feel challenged and positive but not so much that they become distressed. The secret is to be aware of the child's present level of functioning and to work from there in a realistic manner.

Another important guide for parents is not to allow a child to slide out of responsibility. Loving children means encouraging them and being positively firm with them in pursuing the responsible behaviours that will gain them the skills and abilities which will enable them to have an independent, fulfilling and challenging life. Parents cease to love their children when they allow them to slide out of responsibility. But the challenges that are set need to be close to their present level of functioning. If the gap is too wide between their present knowledge and skill levels and what the parent is expecting of them, then children will become anxious and threatened and will resort to the protective strategy either of avoidance or compensation.

It is now well established that without attention to self-esteem children are not likely to make long-term scholastic progress. Research is showing that, in general, people's levels of achievement are influenced by how they see themselves and, more specifically, that self-esteem and academic achievement are strongly associated.

Parents are in the most powerful position to influence how their children feel about themselves. The most important medium of influence the parent has is the relationship with his or her child, and when this is valuing and caring in nature the child's self-esteem will be elevated.

SUICIDE AND ATTEMPTED SUICIDE AMONG THE YOUNG

Michael J. Kelleher

Suicide and attempted suicide are clearly not the same thing. In the one, the individual actively takes his or her own life whereas, in the other, only the minority die by attempted suicide. It is estimated that amongst those who attempt suicide, approximately 15 per cent will go on to die by suicide in the succeeding twenty years. In the first year, the proportion is estimated at being as low as 1 per cent. For this reason, researchers have substituted the word *parasuicide* for attempted suicide. The implication is that the majority of those who engage in such behaviour do not, in fact, intend to end their lives but, rather, to change their immediate circumstances. The effect of such an act, however, can be devastating for their relatives, friends, school-mates and teachers.

Death on the threshold of full adult life is always tragic. The commonest causes of such deaths in Ireland in the past were tuberculosis and cancer. Changes in social policy and advances in medical understanding and care brought about a great reduction in the frequency of deaths from tuberculosis. Better diagnosis and the virtual removal of tuberculosis brought cancer to the forefront as the primary cause of death in young Irish people.

Recent changes, however, over the past two to three decades, have shown startling increases in the frequency of suicide so that as a cause of death in Ireland, amongst young people, suicide is competing with cancer for the primary place. Superficially, it would appear that with cancer the individual has no choice, whereas, with suicide, death is by choice. As ever, however, reality is much more complex than single, simple, human ideas.

The rise in suicide
The first and fundamental question to ask is whether there is a genuine rise in the suicide rate in Ireland. The official suicide rate is probably now in the region of four hundred per annum in the Irish Republic. One study in Cork suggested that the official rate

may underestimate the true rate by a factor of about 15 per cent. In other words, the real rate, as opposed to the official rate, may approach five hundred each year. Studies done in other parts of the country have come up with different figures. In the west of Ireland it has been suggested that there is great under-estimation of the true suicide rate, whereas a study done in Kildare found no under-estimation.

It is certainly true that traditionally the suicide rate in Ireland was genuinely low. Irish migrants to the United States and Australia maintained this low suicide rate. Amongst the immigrant groups studied there, the Irish were the least likely to die by suicide. Furthermore, most if not all countries, tend to have some under-estimation of the true suicide rate and there is no reason why Ireland should be different in this. Reasons for under-estimation have included compassion for relatives and the good name of the deceased, as well as concern, in the past, that those who died by suicide would not be given the full rites of the Church. This might have involved exclusion from a church burial ground or, when such burial was allowed, confinement to the north wall of the graveyard. Christ, who supped with sinners, can hardly be blamed for such inhumanity. More recently, non-payment on insurance policies may have led to the camouflaging of suicide deaths.

The manner of collecting suicide statistics has undoubtedly improved in Ireland over the past thirty years and this may partially explain the rise. The major part of the increase in the official rate, however, is undoubtedly due to a real change in frequency. The suicide rate amongst women may have doubled and that amongst men may have quadrupled in the past thirty years. There is some hope, however, in the fact that over the past ten years the suicide rate among women in Ireland appears to have levelled off. Unfortunately, this is not the case amongst Irish men. Over the past four to five years, there has been a further substantial increase in male suicides. Our current rates are comparable to those of England and Wales, whose figures may now be less reliable than those in Ireland.

The main increase in suicide in Ireland has been amongst young and middle-aged men as well as middle-aged women.

Older Irish people are still relatively protected from suicide. This is not the experience of other countries where there is a serial increase in suicide in each decade of life from the second to the seventh.

Reason for the increase in Irish suicide rates

Most of those who die by suicide are mentally ill during the time before their deaths. The most common illnesses are depression and alcoholism. There is no evidence, however, that the frequency of depression in Ireland has increased over the past thirty years. The situation regarding alcoholism is more difficult to judge. Admission rates for alcoholism have fallen but this may have been due to changes in administrative hospital practice as well as the development of many community-based services for those with problems with alcohol. The amount we spend on alcohol has not diminished and our young people, both boys and girls, are increasingly using alcohol to mark most social events of importance to them, whether celebrating the arrival of Junior or Leaving Cert results or simply attending the local disco.

The reasons for the rise in suicide are much more likely to centre on social and psychological considerations rather than on illness itself. Put differently, the distressed young person today is much more likely to consider suicide as a solution than a similar youngster was thirty years ago.

Ireland has seen many changes over the past three decades. Research done in other countries has demonstrated that the fragmentation of society, or the loosening of its traditional bonds, is associated with an increase in suicide. These changes ultimately affect family life. We all emerge from families and most of us create new ones. An increase in suicide is associated with a fall in the marriage rate, a rise in the numbers of children born outside wedlock, in the alcoholism rate and in the crime rate. The increase in suicide in Ireland, as in other countries, has been similarly associated. It is not that the one social change directly causes the other but, rather, rapid or excessive individualisation carries an increased risk of death by suicide, even if suicide itself is still a comparatively rare phenomenon. About one in ten thousand Irish people dies by suicide each year.

There are many other changes in Irish society which may have a direct bearing upon suicide. Church attendance in all Christian denominations has diminished. This fall-off is not evenly spread through the age groups. Children, the middle aged and the elderly are the most loyal to traditional church practice. Adolescents and young adults generally attend less frequently. There are also differences between urban and rural areas and within urban areas, and between the middle classes and the poor. Furthermore, amongst those attending third-level institutions, the frequency of practice may be lower than amongst the non-student body of the same age group. It is true, however, that no one knows precisely the extent of these changes although the question has been carefully addressed in a recent pan-European study.

To the extent that fall-off in church attendance reflects a fundamental change in religious value and commitment, it is likely to be important in influencing suicide. Traditionally, Christian life was ever conscious of the four last things beloved of medieval Christian writing. These were death, judgment, heaven and hell. The only certainty remaining in most people's eyes is death itself. The hereafter is either not discussed or apologetically questioned. Judgment, if it exists, is assumed to be benign. Both heaven and hell are reduced in status or conceptualised as a state of mind of more importance to the living than to the dead.

Morally, the tendency is to see suicide as a neutral act in itself. Any immorality attaching to it is seen as being determined by the failure to honour social obligations to others rather than seeing the bringing about of one's own death as wrong. These changes in social attitude are more predominant in some continental European countries such as Holland than they are yet in Ireland. Nevertheless, our collective psyche is changing. All hinges on whether individual life is in itself sacred. If it is sacred, as I believe it is, then the act of suicide is inherently wrong, irrespective of its effects on others. If, on the other hand, human life is not sacred, then the individual has the right to do with it as he or she will, provided he or she does not do harm to others, in particular his or her relatives, friends and school-mates.

Traditional Christian values and practices offered many

things. Amongst them was an attempt to give an explanation of and a philosophy for living with the pain which is never far from human existence. The anodyne of alcohol and drugs has a high association with suicide. One German writer has described these addictive practices as suicide by instalment. Many suicides in Ireland are associated with the ingestion of alcohol, which may be taken to reduce anxiety prior to the self-destructive act. In one study of young male suicides, virtually all had taken alcohol before they killed themselves.

Most of those who take their lives are ambivalent about the act. It is often chance and the selection of method which determines outcome. The importance of this, however, is that most of those who attempt suicide do not die by suicide. This places a very clear obligation on society to prevent such acts and to extend specialised treatment to those who make an attempt.

Whose fault is suicide?

In the past society blamed the individual. Roman law dealt particularly harshly with slaves who attempted to kill themselves. The act was seen as a form of theft in which the master was deprived of a service for which he had already paid. In selling a slave, the vendor had an obligation to disclose suicidal tendencies, particularly if the act had been attempted. In the case of soldiers, the act was regarded as treacherous.

The victim's family were punished and unless it could be shown that the deceased had lost his reason, they were deprived of all his material possessions. St Augustine, responding to the Donatist heresy, adopted a similar approach. He took the view that those who, in a clear mind, purposely ended their lives, were excluded from the sight of God. The Donatist had favoured ending this life's existence early with a view to entering the kingdom of heaven.

Today, however, people are much more likely to blame society than the individual. Unemployment is one such candidate for blame. It is not a simple question, however. There are many causes of unemployment and some of these may predispose the individual to suicide. The threat of job loss, the response to redundancy and poor working conditions and relationships may be much more important than unemployment itself. Many of those who take their lives are in fact employed, and many others, on the surface, have high employment potential. Nevertheless, they choose to die.

Exam pressure and the points system are a further focus of attention in endeavouring to understand suicide amongst the young. There have been several notorious suicides among examinees who did not achieve their often self-imposed goals. The danger of media attention in these matters has also been highlighted. Example is a terrible thing. The young and the vulnerable are shaped by the models given them by the communications industry.

It is argued that we in Ireland need a press council to act as a self-imposed watch-dog for harmful reporting. Such an office exists in Britain but it did not prevent the high profile given to a young woman who, having recovered from a near fatal riding accident, ultimately ended her life when she failed to get her desired professional placement. Work done in America and Germany, as well as Britain, has shown that such reporting is almost invariably followed by an increase in suicide in succeeding weeks.

In Ireland, however, the press, particularly the national press, is more responsible. The issue at stake is a simple one. Individual suicides should never be reported in the media in a manner which glorifies the act and thereby leads others in similar circumstances to follow suit. Reporting on trends, i.e. group patterns of suicide, does not seem to have the same effect. The latter is necessary because it is essential that society face the suicide problem directly and endeavours to reduce both its frequency and its harmful effects. We are unlikely to do this unless the data is available to everyone. It is not simply a matter for doctors.

Many pop idols do give bad example. They often project the distress of their own private lives through their art. A few speak openly about suicide and some have incorporated it into their music and song. All of this trivialises life, and the mesmeric effect may, like the Pied Piper, lead some into an early death. Education can protect people against these negative influences.

Self-poisoning and deliberate self-harm

For every completed suicide in Ireland, there are between ten and twenty attempted suicides. In other words, there are between five and ten thousand attempted suicides in Ireland each year.

Unlike completed suicides, there is no way of establishing the true figure. Research carried out in Cork over the past fifteen years or so has shown, however, that both the number of attempts and the number of individuals attempting has increased each year since 1982. The cost to the health services, to the individuals involved, to their families and acquaintances, is huge.

As with suicide, there are multiple causes rather than a single one. Deprivation, particularly social deprivation, characterises many who engage in this harmful sort of human behaviour. The highest rates tend to occur in those coming from poor areas with minimal education, no employment, over-crowded housing and with a family and personal background of illness, including depression, anxiety, alcoholism and benzodiazepine dependency. Many have also suffered gross trauma in childhood, including physical and sexual abuse. The scales of the balance of life are tilted against them from the beginning.

There are schools in Ireland where the majority of the children have parents who are out of work and who face a future without employment. Work serves many functions of which the economic is only one. It is also a source of status, social meaning and purpose, as well as a conduit through which new relationships are channelled and recreational pursuits are developed. Removing this prospect encourages passivity, dependency and reactivity. When frustration mounts, acts of deliberate self-poisoning and deliberate self-harm may follow.

Those who have been empowered through education may redirect their frustration into creative activities which ultimately lead to a positive change in their social milieu. The deprived and inadequately educated are less likely to have such a resource. They may respond more frequently with acts of aggression directed towards those in their immediate environment or, on occasion, with similar acts perpetrated against themselves.

Deprived and non-deprived areas differ in many ways. A key difference is often where the employed leaders of the society –

teachers, politicians, doctors, police officers – live. Such people are much more likely to reside outside, rather than inside, the deprived areas which they serve. The clergy are still the one exception to this general rule.

What should Ireland do about the problem?

In Ireland and England the Coroner's Court, dating from Norman times, is one of the oldest judicial offices in the land. As the name implies, this functionary was appointed by the king. The coroner's function in the case of suicide was to determine the circumstances of the death and whether the individual intended to take his or her life. If he or she did so in clear mind, i.e. in the absence of profound loss of reason, then his or her goods and possessions were forfeited by an almoner, even if they may not always have reached the royal coffers. For these material reasons, the verdict of suicide and the mental state of the deceased has always provoked interest.

Today, Irish coroners avoid the word suicide but their description of the manner of the person's death is usually clear-cut and informative. This, together with a special form filled out by the Gardaí, and other information, is used by the Central Statistics Office to determine whether unnatural deaths have been due to suicide, accident or misadventure. These figures provide a body of important information for the researcher. It is likely, however, that the figures could be put to much better use.

It would not be a difficult matter to assemble a small, expert committee who would review the suicide figures annually, as well as their attendant causes and methods. The coroners as a body would favour such an approach. If this suggestion were implemented, then each year Irish society would be in a situation to recommend specific changes which might result in a fall in suicide rates.

Two simple examples spring to mind. Each year an increasing and significant minority end their lives by ingesting paracetamol tablets which are freely available, without prescription, in pharmacies, supermarkets and local stores. There is no restriction on how many may be purchased. The difference between the therapeutic dose and the harmful dose is not great. Furthermore, this substance forms part of many other medicinal compounds which can be purchased without medical advice. To add to the problem many of those who ingest the substance and do not die do in fact injure their livers. Some have had to have liver transplants, the cost of which may be very substantial. An inroad into this single cause of injury and death could be made by restricting the availability of both quantity and outlet. If it was decided that prescription was not necessary, then sale could be confined to chemist shops where there would be an obligation on the chemist to enquire for what purpose the tablets were to be used.

A further infrequent but increasingly used method of suicide in Ireland, although much more common in Britain, is carbon monoxide poisoning from car exhaust fumes. Two simple measures would reduce this: firstly, catalytic converters, which result in fewer toxic fumes being emitted by the engine; secondly, changing the shape of the exhaust so that it would not be easy to fit a hosepipe over it.

Those who argue in favour of doing nothing on the grounds that if a person does not have access to one method, he or she will choose another, are misinformed. In Britain, the change from coal gas, which is highly toxic, to natural gas, which is much less so, has been associated with a fall in the suicide rate. Suicide and attempted suicide, particularly amongst the young, has a cohort effect. In other words, if a person grows out of the vulnerable age group, then chances of suicide lessen. This is similar to what happens in relation to criminality. The majority of prisoners are young people but most people are imprisoned only once.

The cost to society of suicide and parasuicide is enormous. One estimate has been that the EU spends over six billion pounds each year as a result of completed suicides. No one knows how much is spent in responding to parasuicide. With such financial losses, it might be supposed that comparable resources would be allocated to research in this area.

Up to now, however, this has not been the case, although a grant was made recently, indicating recognition at least of the need for a better understanding of this growing problem.

Specific helping agencies

The Samaritans provide a twenty-four-hour, confidential, non-professional listening ear on the telephone and, in some areas, in particular cases, face-to-face consultations. Most people who contact the Samaritans are distressed. Some make a habit of contacting them. There is no doubt but that the Samaritans answer a real need within society. The fragmentation of our social life is compensated by these voluntary workers.

Their influence, however, in reducing both suicide and deliberate self-harm is less apparent. Lest this be seen as a criticism of the excellent work done, it should be immediately added that the professionals in this area, even though they have increased in number and are perhaps better educated, have had no significant effect on the upward drift of these phenomena. Fortunately, the leaders of the Samaritans movement are pragmatic and well-disposed towards both research and the possibility of improving all services, both statutory and voluntary. In projected future research work within Cork and Kerry, the Samaritans will play an important part.

Sudden death is always a shock and a tragedy for which relatives and friends are rarely prepared. This is particularly so in the case of suicide. The Friends of the Suicide Bereaved are active in Cork and Dublin and they offer support and understanding to those bereaved in this way. In doing so, they provide a further valuable caring service.

Ireland has many other voluntary groups who give their time and attention to helping those distressed by psychological illness. Amongst these are the Mental Welfare Association, AWARE, GROW, and the Schizophrenia Association. There are also groups for other conditions such as Alcoholics Anonymous, Narcotics Anonymous and Gamblers Anonymous. Added to these, there are other voluntary groups and community associations, including the Society of St Vincent de Paul, which endeavours to reduce the burden of everyday living for those unequal to the tasks imposed upon them by life. Each of these helps in its own way, even though none was founded specifically to reduce suicide or deliberate self-harm.

Has the school and education a part to play?

Education ought to prepare children for adult life in all its varieties. The school is only part of this preparation. Neither parents nor society has the right to devolve upon the school the sole responsibility for preparing our young for adulthood. Nevertheless, the school and those who organise its curriculum, both centrally and locally, have a great responsibility.

Earlier it was implied that the points system in itself is not a cause of suicide. Yet the points system, by providing a narrow focus, impoverishes the lives of young people. All of us, including the young themselves, their teachers and their parents, become part of this constricted vision.

Adult life is changing. Although a significant majority of our young people will never have a full-time job which will last for more than five years, they are prepared both at second level and third level as if their choice of career was permanent and indelible. Some, also, are imbued with the idea that occupation is everything, although the four-day week is not far away.

Furthermore, the number of years spent in employment, for most, is diminishing. One effect of third-level education is to reduce the years of active gainful employment. Technological change often results in men and women in their early or mid-forties ceasing to be members of the work-force. The distinction between schooling, working and retirement continues to blur. Yet each crop of youth is sent through the same educational gates as their parents before them, even though their working lives will bear little resemblance to what their parents experienced.

It is also possible today that boys are being, in an odd way, discriminated against. It is right that all careers and all professions are thrown open to girls. Girls, however, have retained habits and abilities relating to everyday living which boys do not acquire, either at home or in school. Take the case of the great economic depression of sixty years ago in the United States. Although it fell equally on women as well as men, and although, in the order of things, women may have been more greatly affected economically as their menfolk controlled the household budget, yet the psychological consequences of being forced to leave the work-force were attested to be far greater amongst the men than amongst the women. The men's education had prepared them for employment and not for idleness. There are domestic and recreational skills, as well as attitudes, which boys need to acquire if they are to be successful in accommodating to the vicissitudes of life, including the unlikelihood of continuous employment.

Perhaps the most important asset for any young person is a sense of dignity and self-worth. As infants and young children, how do we see ourselves as we emerge from the parental world? We see ourselves reflected in the gaze of our parents and of our teachers. If they reflect warmth and acceptance, we accept ourselves in a spirit of warmth and security. Deep criticism in these early formative years wounds and may kill. Love enables and frees the human spirit.

What should schools do?
The school must give more than the three R's or the modern equivalents, important though these are. The child needs a wider preparation for life. Some schools, in other countries, have sought to reverse suicide and deliberate self-harm trends by giving specific addresses to high school students. The effect is often the opposite to what is intended. Although the intention was undoubtedly good, these interventions have been associated with an increase in frequencies of deliberate self-harm.

The results might have been different had the voluntary educators spoken about other important topics such as the need to moderate drinking habits, the need to avoid drug-taking and the importance of coming to terms with one's own emotional life. Depression and anxiety are common personal experiences. Most of us overcome them, through trial and error, without the need for professional help.

School children and adolescents have their own special age-related emotional problems. Their education at school should include discussion of mechanisms for overcoming these from within their own resources of personality and their own private social worlds. If such discussion were more freely available, then perhaps rates of suicide and parasuicide would fall. But, even if they did not, there is, nevertheless, an important need that ought to be fulfilled in these modern terms. The American doctor who researched this area with the greatest thoroughness was recently asked at a symposium on suicide in Cork how one should intervene within the school system. His advice was specific. It centred on case identification and the referral of people at risk to the appropriate professional person with the cooperation of parents or guardians. In a class of twenty-five teenaged students, it can be assumed that at least two are going through a difficult, emotional time. This may become apparent in different ways. A change in behaviour is one, either a fall-off in work performance, social withdrawal or unruly behaviour out of character for him or her. Another way is through what is written in essays. For example, a boy who conveys a morbid attitude towards life and living through what he writes and says in class, should be seen privately by the teacher and by a counsellor in order to clarify what is truly within his mind. If in doubt, the teacher, being in *loco parentis,* should contact the parent, if possible with the student's permission.

It is important for schools and for school authorities that their system should be right even if, as in medicine, the best system is beyond coping with the unexpected vagaries of individual human behaviour. However, if there is a safety net in place within the school, then the school cannot be held responsible for any tragedy that occurs, whether amongst its gymnasts or amongst its emotionally unstable students. Each school should have an energetic counsellor of suitable personality who is readily available to the students. Such a person may also give advice on careers, taking into consideration what is available and what the student's potential is. Most of us, as adults, are grateful to individual teachers, who by their example and access to us as children, had an inspirational effect on our adult lives.

Conclusion

Human existence is a gift. We do not create ourselves but, rather, if we are lucky, we discover ourselves and come to realise the finiteness of our individual life. We live through more than seven ages in our passage across the decades. To terminate our lives before its completion is much like a skipper scuttling his ship. Suicide should be looked at in the same way. Most of those who are interrupted in the act of suicide never complete the event.

EDUCATION AND THE FAMILY: THEIR ROLE IN PREVENTING (OR CREATING) JUVENILE OFFENDERS

Peter McVerry SJ

A true story

John is now serving his third prison sentence for robbery. He was the eldest of nine children with both parents alcoholics. John's early childhood and schooling were frequently disrupted due to the eviction of his parents from their local authority housing for non-payment of rent. Each time John settled into school, got to know the teacher and made friends in class, he was suddenly pulled out and moved to another school in another area. John learned how to defend himself against the pain of parting – not to make friends and keep his distance from the teacher. Eventually, the family were re-housed in the most run-down housing available, in an area where no-one wanted to live because of the many 'problem' families who had been 'dumped' there, and, consequently, the myriad social problems which existed in the neighbourhood.

John frequently went to school without breakfast as there was little food in the house. Each night he waited for his parents to come in from the pub drunk. Frequently they would argue and fight till the early hours of the morning. During those fights all the children were awakened and were often physically beaten. By the age of nine, John's attendance at school was very poor. A fierce Alsatian dog kept school attendance officers and Gardaí from calling too frequently! By the age of twelve, John had simply dropped out of school and no-one noticed. He spent his days and most of his nights on the streets in the company of older boys who were robbing. By the age of fourteen, John was well known to the Gardaí and local judiciary. He went to live in a hostel where he got on well with the staff and other boys and did reasonably well. From time to time, he would disappear for several weeks: he was out robbing to get the money to re-connect the electricity in his parents' house, or to buy Christmas presents for the younger children. Sometimes he was just too depressed to stick the discipline and order of the hostel and he went back to the streets, robbing to survive. But they were the happiest and most positive years of his life. They just came too late.

At the age of seventeen, he left the hostel, now too old for the – to him – childish rules and requirements which were intended for younger boys. He had nowhere to go except the over-crowd-ed home of his alcoholic parents or back to the streets. Either way, it was back to robbing, starting on drugs and into jail.

John's story may read like a Roddy Doyle novel, but sadly it is a true story (with the name changed). It is all too typical of many of the young offenders with whom I am in contact.

Causes of juvenile crime

For centuries now, people have asked themselves the question, 'What are the causes of juvenile crime?' The answer, given by a large majority, is invariably 'the parents'. Today, the increasing break-up of families, a large rise in the number of single-parent families, the increased tendency for mothers to find paid employment outside the home or the drinking habits of parents are all blamed for the problem. Poverty and educational failure are often seen as alternative, or at least complementary, causes. A vast amount of research – though, sadly, very little in Ireland – has been conducted on the subject of juvenile crime, often with little agreement as to the cause. This article seeks to identify some of the links between family, education and juvenile offending on which this research reaches some degree of agreement. This may then shed some light on the possibility of predicting which chil-dren are likely to becomes juvenile offenders and what type of intervention might be most effective.

One problem posed by the question 'What are the causes of juvenile crime?' is how to clarify what we mean by 'juvenile crime' and to evolve an accurate but reasonably simple way of measuring criminal behaviour. For example, if we confine ourselves to 'official' records, i.e. Garda statistics for arrest, caution and conviction, the problem may be complicated by different Garda attitudes and responses to juvenile offenders in deprived and in middle-class areas. Again, agreement on what constitutes a 'juvenile offender' may differ. For example, does an isolated incident of drunk and disorderly behaviour justify the classification of a juvenile as an offender? Is a middle-class teenager who 'borrows' his father's car to bring his friends to a party the same as a teenager from a deprived area who 'borrows' someone else's car to get home after the last bus has gone? In fact, every young person growing up commits some crime at some stage in their development, but a 'clip on the ear' (no longer permissible) or being confined to their room was usually an appropriate and adequate response. By juvenile offender I mean a young person who has been involved in two or more incidents of serious anti-social or criminal behaviour such as burglary or acts of violence.

An analysis of our introductory story about John above will identify a series of factors usually associated with juvenile delinquency. Together, they form a path down which many young offenders travel.

Seriously dysfunctional family Blaming the parents may not be the appropriate response and, indeed, may make the situation even worse. In John's case, the parents went through considerable periods of sobriety, especially when intensive support was available to them.

Poor education It was impossible for John to succeed at school, often arriving tired, hungry and late, often not being woken for school in the morning at all, always trying to cope with what had happened the night before and worried about what was going to happen the night after.

Low self-esteem By the age of nine, John felt he was a failure. He was a drop-out, different from the other boys who went to school each day and actually – unbelievable to John – seemed to be happy!

Failure to integrate It was only one short step from John's belief that he was no good to a belief that no-one liked him, wanted him, cared about him, or was interested in him.

Sense of alienation John came to live in a different world from the majority of those around him, a world apart, a world of alienation. The aspirations, hopes and values of his world had little in common with the world around him.

Anti-Social and Offending Behaviour John's interaction with the larger world around him was primarily one of conflict - on both sides. Could society have intervened in John's life in an earlier and more effective way that might have kept him out of prison? We first need to ask if it is possible to identify those who are at risk of becoming offenders and what signs should we look for.

Research

The following conclusions about the predictability of future criminal behaviour have been drawn from some of the research available:

• Offenders tend to be those who had earlier been identified at primary school as impulsive, aggressive, troublesome, unpopular and dishonest. Their intelligence and attainment scores were lower than average.

• Neither the father's occupational status, nor having a mother who worked, were related to later delinquency. But future offenders were more likely to have been part of low-income and larger families, to have lived in run-down housing, to have received help from the social services and to have shown signs of physical neglect by their parents.

• Experience of divorce or parental separation before the age of ten was associated with future delinquency, as was conflict between parents in the home.

• Parents whose child-rearing practices included harsh or erratic discipline, a cruel, passive or neglecting attitude, and poor overall supervision were more likely to produce delinquent teenagers.

• Children were more likely to grow into delinquency if one or both parents had a background of offending or if they had an older sibling who was delinquent.

In short, the four most important predictors of future offending were:

1. Economic deprivation
2. Family criminality
3. Parental mishandling
4. School failure

If a youngster combined three out of the above four, the future was ominous. It seems clear then that the two major interventions which can most influence future behaviour are the school and the parents.

The role of education in preventing delinquency
Schools are of paramount importance in any crime prevention strategy for young people.

1. *Pre-school*

> It would be an act of political courage to invest substantially in services for pre-school children in the belief that it would relieve spending on services for delinquency later in life. (Social Information Services Ltd, an independent UK consultancy agency)

Pre-school education is integral to preventive measures. Research demonstrates that children who take part in quality pre-school programmes receive an educational advantage that makes them more receptive learners once they embark on compulsory schooling, thus extending the influence of pre-school into adolescence and increasing their chances of employment success and decreasing risks of delinquency. Quality pre-school programmes are ones with a low pupil-teacher ratio (10:1 or less), with a close working relationship between the teachers and parents and where the children are encouraged to plan their own play and take responsibility for their activities. This latter criterion is considered especially important for any delinquency prevention effects.

Good pre-school education is not just about educating children but is equally about involving, motivating and engaging parents. Involving parents as helpers in the classroom has been found to be one of the strongest predictors of a child's future school success (and consequently possible future delinquent behaviour). France, Belgium and Italy have between 88 and 95 per cent of all 3-5 year olds in pre-school education, Britain has 46 per cent, the US has 20 per cent (National Children's Bureau, 1990). The percentage of children in Ireland attending pre-school education is unknown, to the best of my knowledge.

Although pre-school education has enduring benefits which are directly or indirectly relevant to preventing delinquency, it obviously does not reach its potential in isolation. The increased improvements in parental competence, motivation and aspirations may be relatively short-lived if parental involvement ceases at primary or secondary level.

2. *Primary school*

One of the best predictors of later delinquency, in the case of boys, has been found to be the rating of their troublesomeness at age 8-10 by teachers and classmates.

Primary school education is now considered more important in affecting delinquency than was once thought. School failure is linked with delinquency through its impact on self-esteem and the formation of anti-school peer groups. The most significant influence in improving a child's performance in school and, therefore, their ability to take advantage of educational opportunity was found to be the parents' attitude to education and interest in school work. Those schools that fostered and encouraged such participation by the parents had significantly lower delinquency rates even when the pupil intake was similar to other schools.

3. *Post-primary school*

It is during second-level schooling that pupil disaffection is most likely to manifest itself in truancy, anti-social behaviour, educational under-performance and offending. For example, persistent non-attendance at second-level schooling is associated with juvenile and later adult offending. John Graham of the Helsinki Institute for Crime Prevention and Control states the research findings simply:

> Schools which are likely to have high rates of delinquency among pupils are those which, inadvertently or otherwise, segregate pupils according to academic ability; concentrate on academic success at the expense of practical and social skills, categorise pupils as deviants, inadequates and failures and refer responsibility for the behaviour and welfare of their pupils to outside agencies and institutions. Schools

which permanently exclude their most difficult pupils or ignore those who persistently fail to attend school may themselves be contributing to the promotion of delinquency. (John Graham, 1990, for the Helsinki Institute for Crime Prevention and Control).

On the other hand, certain post-primary schools help prevent juvenile delinquency:

Those schools which are able to offer students a sense of achievement regardless of ability and are able to motivate and integrate them are likely to reduce the incidence of negative outcomes. (John Graham, op. cit.)

Parents have diminishing influence over their children at secondary school age due to their increased independence and the growing tendency to accept the behavioural values of their chosen peer group. It is also more difficult to foster a good relationship between home and school. At this age, most parents are unaware of their importance to the secondary school process and are more inclined to leave the education of their children solely to the teachers. The traditional, more formal, parent-teacher meetings tend to be dominated by the parents of more successful children. Schools which promote more informal contact, seek out and encourage parents who would not normally show an interest in their children's secondary schooling, and are careful about explaining policies to parents, can reduce delinquent behaviour. As contact between parents and school at secondary level tend to be less frequent than at primary or pre-school level, it is all the more important that this contact be quality contact – personal, individual and informal.

Parental influence

It is clear from our research that problem children tend to grow into problem adults and that problem adults tend to reproduce problem children. Sooner or later, serious efforts, firmly grounded on empirical research results, must be made to break this cycle. (Farrington D.P. and D.J. West on the Cambridge Study Project).

Parental influence is clearly recognised as the single most important factor in determining children's future behavioural patterns. The vast majority of parents, including parents of offending children, want to do their best for their children. In some cases, their best may not be good enough.

The rate of delinquency in homes where parental supervision was lax was much higher than for families assessed as being strict. Parental supervision of pre-teen children was the most important single factor in determining juvenile delinquency:

> Large family size and overcrowding lead to unsupervised play in streets and yards and early severance of mother-child contact affects behavioural training. Children learn to adapt by developing techniques of aggression and withdrawal. …Lax supervision in this setting is not a deliberate choice of a permissive style of parenting; it carries an element of abandonment. (Harriett Wilson, West Midlands Survey)

For older children, however, the parental supervision factor was modified by the choice of peer group friends: If children associated with a delinquent peer group, it makes little difference to their own behaviour whether their activities appear to be well or poorly monitored by their parents.

Thus, for pre-teen children, the level of parental supervision is very strongly related to future behaviour, while for older children, the influence of their parents diminishes and the influence of their peer group increases. Clearly, the two are related as those who have been least well supervised by their parents when young are more likely to mix with the 'wrong crowd' of other anti-social children. In other words, the power of parents in a crime prevention context is at its greatest before their children reach the age of ten.

> Parenthood today is a demanding and at times stressful, lonely and frustrating experience, and if society continues to put expectations on parents, then it must also provide sufficient support to enable them to fulfil their obligations with knowledge, understanding and enjoyment. (Gillian Pugh and Erica D'Aeth, 1984).

Parent education

A comprehensive approach to parent education, extending from sex education classes and 'preparation for family life' classes in school, to support services for the parents of turbulent teenagers would reduce the level of juvenile offending more significantly than any other single measure. Such support services should emphasise the need for men to make shared parenting a reality. It is especially important that parental education programmes do not stigmatise those families at risk (because this may unwittingly help the self-fulfilling process), but are available to all, particularly in areas of deprivation. Regretfully, such classes are not yet part of the educational curriculum and Health Boards have not had the resources to provide adequate support services for parents, particularly in those areas that needed them most. However, the Child Care Act of 1991 makes explicit provision for family support services by the Health Boards, directly or by arrangements with voluntary bodies. But, at this point in time, the resources made available to implement the Child Care Act 1991 have been woefully inadequate.

The lack of a coherent national strategy on parent education and parent support services is perhaps the most serious obstacle to tackling the problem of juvenile crime.

I have argued in this article that a coherent strategy for preventing juvenile offending should focus on two principal areas: educating and supporting parents and improving educational opportunities for children, especially in deprived neighbourhoods.

A new Juvenile Justice Bill is about to be produced by the Department of Justice. It provides an ideal opportunity to legislate for such measures. Unfortunately, it may well focus on punishing parents for their children's behaviour and providing further custodial or semi-custodial education where parental involvement is minimal. In the absence of adequate research programme into juvenile crime in Ireland, such measures may appear to be reasonable and would certainly be politically popular. Their effect in preventing and reducing juvenile offending will, however, be virtually nil.

THE ETHOS OF A SCHOOL: A CULTURAL ANALYSIS APPROACH

Tom O'Keeffe and J. Matthew Feheney FPM

> We shall not cease from exploration
> and the end of all our exploring
> will be to arrive where we started
> and know the place for the first time.[1]

On entering a school for the first time a person quickly obtains a general impression of its ethos, as much, perhaps, through intuition as through the signs and symbols one observes: the trophy cabinets, statues, pictures and photographs, the behaviour of the pupils and staff and the welcome extended by the Principal - all manifestations of the ethos of the school. Indeed, many would argue that ethos requires external manifestations to grow and develop. Thus, Handy and Aitken contend that the ethos of a school 'needs to be articulated, not just in the formal prose of the school's prospectus, but in the everyday utterances and behaviour of its members ... it needs its outward and visible signs.'[2]

The terms 'climate', 'atmosphere' and 'spirit' are sometimes used as synonyms of 'ethos'. Even a cursory perusal of educational literature will reveal other related, if not synonymous, words: 'tone', 'genius' and 'character'. One writer, Williams, defines ethos as 'the dominant pervading spirit or character of a school ... the hidden curriculum ... part of the fabric of our being.'[3]

There is not a little uncertainty about, dissatisfaction with and criticism of the imprecise nature of such terms as 'climate', 'spirit' and 'atmosphere'.[4] With this in mind, and in keeping with the trends in writing on organisation theory and educational administration, the more encompassing term 'school culture' will be used in preference to 'school ethos' in this paper. This is not a novel suggestion since some existing studies treat 'ethos' and 'culture' as 'very similar concepts' within the context of school.[5] We will further suggest that the analysis of the culture of a school is an easier, more manageable and, possibly, more rewarding task than the articulation of its own special ethos.

Culture as a root metaphor

In the past fifteen years or so, educational writing (Handy and Aitken, Deal and Kennedy, Beare *et al*, for example), drawing on research related to large organisations and business conglomerates, has focused on the culture of schools. Peters and Waterman, in one of many references, point to the importance of the culture of organisations: 'Without exception, the dominance and coherence of culture proved to be an essential quality of the excellent companies.'[6]

In administrative science, organisations have long been characterised as machine – well oiled – or as organism – adapting to changing environments. However, new interest in the micro-study of organisations has shown new posssibilities for the use of an old, but powerful metaphor, culture. Jelinek and associates, writing in *Administrative Science Quarterly*, put it this way:

New ideas in and of themselves are and can be valuable. Culture as a root metaphor for organisation studies is one such idea, redirecting our attention away from some of the commonly accepted 'important things' (such as structure or technology) and towards the (until now) less frequently examined elements raised to importance by the new metaphor (such as shared understandings, norms or values).[7]

Thus, many writers in this area have adopted the term 'culture' to define the social and phenomenological uniqueness of a particular group.[8] Every organisation is different: every school is different from every other school. This is only to be expected since organisations are living things, unique entities made up of intangible and symbolic elements (values, philosophies, ideologies), as well as the more tangible (audible, visible and behavioural).

Porous boundaries

There cannot be a culture unless there is a group that 'owns' it. Culture is embedded in groups and, by dealing with the culture of the school, we automatically embrace the concept of schools as social organisations. This, according to the authors of some significant studies of schools, is helpful. Thus, Rutter suggests that, 'By introducing the concept of an ethos, we mean that it is valuable to think of schools in terms of their characteristics as social organisations.'[9] Handy (1986) takes the same view. Schools comprise people: their activities are, for the most part, people-oriented and people-centred. Furthermore, the purpose of the school is people development and each individual makes a unique personal contribution to the particular school. We can regard these participating people as agents of the culture.

The agents of culture can be divided into two groups: primary and secondary. The primary agents include the principal, vice-principal, middle management, teachers and students. Each primary agent, in turn, is influenced by a group of secondary agents though they, themselves, are not directly involved in the daily life of the school. Among the secondary agents influencing the school administration, for instance, would be the trustees, board of management, Department of Education, local clergy, parents council, past pupils union, teachers union(s), third-level educational institutions, other schools in the catchment area, the media and the business community.

Secondary agents influencing the school staff include those listed above together with their own families, while additional groups influencing the students include their families, peer groups and employers – in the case of those who have a part-time job.

Schools, as social organisations, are open systems in constant interaction with their many environments. We can term these environments the instruments of culture. They provide the raw materials for the agenda of interaction with the agents of culture and include: the educational philosophy of the school; the school tradition with all its implications, including manifestations of core beliefs and values handed on from one generation to the next; the examination system; the discipline code; the enrolment policy; the pastoral care programme, which might be termed the human face of the school culture; the co-curricular programmes; school rituals, myths and symbols; and, of course, the curriculum.

All school boundaries, both internal and external, are highly porous. Having porous external boundaries means that it is not possible for the school to be isolated from sources of influence in the wider cultural and social environment in which it is located, a point to which we shall return later. Conversely, school influences can filter out into the wider community in a variety of ways. The porous nature of internal boundaries implies that each group within the school, be they pupils, teachers or school administrators, will inevitably influence and be influenced by the attitudes, values and behaviour patterns of all the other groups.

Culture

Culture exists at different levels, for example, western culture, Irish culture and, in our case, school culture. Cultural analysis is complicated since the term culture is a very elusive concept which can be used in a variety of ways. We will briefly consider a few of the contexts in which the word 'culture' is used. First, there is the common use of the word in the phrase 'a cultured person', culture here being equated with the fine arts. Culture in this sense is derived from the Latin *cultura*, implying a cultivation or improvement of the quality or life of a person through experience and education. It implies exposure to and acquaintance with art, music and literature – what Matthew Arnold called 'the very best humans' have thought and said. Culture here refers to the wonderful heritage which we have acquired across the ages: what W.B. Yeats termed, 'monuments of (the mind's) magnificence'.[10] Schools have, in fact, preserved this approach to culture in many of their policies and practices over the years and it is often woven into mission statements, prospectuses and codes of discipline.

The *Pastoral Constitution on the Church in the Modern World* (*Gaudium et spes*) uses the word culture in a broader sense. It refers to culture as that which

> ...indicates all the factors by which people refine and unfold their manifold spiritual and bodily qualities. It means their efforts to labour. It includes the fact that by improving customs and institutions, they render social life

more human both within the family and in the civic community.[11]

Culture here is the progress towards the betterment of human society. The Incarnation, the Christ event, gives a divine guarantee to the human enterprise and gives an added dimension to culture.

Anthropologists use the word culture in yet another sense. Culture for them is concerned with human living and understanding – the human enterprise to give meaning to people's daily lives and to satisfy their basic needs in a particular physical and social environment. In one of the earlier definitions of culture, Tylor suggested that it was the 'complete whole which includes knowledge, beliefs, art, morals, laws, customs and any other capabilities or habits acquired by man as a member of society.'[12]

Taking much the same approach, Kluckhohn has described culture as

> ... way of thinking, feeling, believing. It is the knowledge stored up (in the memories of men, in objects and books) for future use: patterns for doing certain things in certain ways ... Culture, then, is one facet of human life which is learned as a result of belonging to some group.[13]

We might, therefore, by way of summary, borrow the definition of an Irish writer who described culture as 'the sum total of knowledge, attitudes and habitual behaviour patterns shared and transmitted by members of a particular society.'[14]

All these descriptions or definitions list elements and aspects of culture, including school culture, such as art, morals, knowledge, sharing, transmitting attitudes and behaviour and belonging to a group. All these reflect the organisation's culture, but none of them adequately describes what culture is. With the interactive model of the school in mind, and using Aristotle's definition of ethos as the 'ethos of what actually goes on',[15] Schein's definition of organisational culture will be found more helpful in understanding school culture. He describes organisational culture as

The pattern of basic assumptions that a given group has

invented, discovered or developed in learning to cope with its problems of external adaptation and internal integration, and that have worked well enough to be considered valid, and, therefore, to be taught to new members as the correct way to perceive, think and feel in relation to those problems.[16]

Using the model in fig. 1, Schein goes on to outline how organisational culture can be analysed at different levels. If the

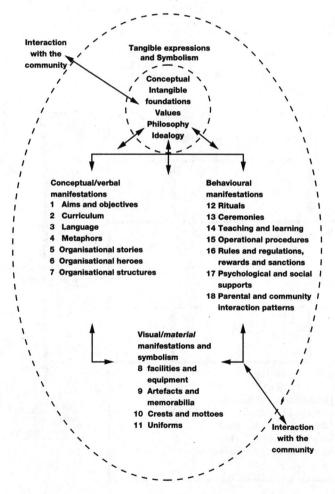

Fig. 1 *Schein's Model*

above discussion of school culture is linked to the models of Schein (fig. 1), Beare (fig. 2) and Flynn (fig. 3), an even more helpful framework for cultural analysis will be obtained. It will be noted from figure 1 that Schein distinguishes the three elements by treating basic assumptions as the essence – what culture really is – and by treating values and behaviours as observed manifestations of that cultural essence. These are levels of culture that can be distinguished and that can lead to a deeper understanding of the concept as applied to organisations and, in our case, to schools.

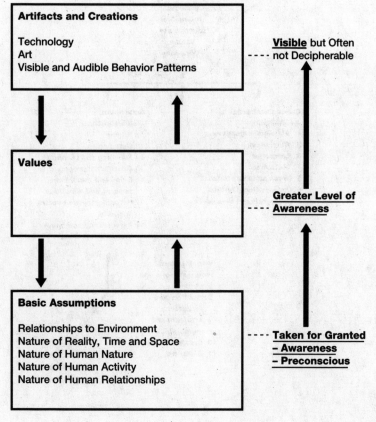

Fig. 2 Model of Beare et al

Level 1: Artifacts and creations

The most visible and superficial level of culture is its artifacts and creations, 'its constructed physical and social environment .. its architecture, manner of dress, visible and audible behaviour patterns and public documents such as charters, employee orientation materials, stories.'[17] Some of these can also be found in schools. Thus, in place of Schein's 'artifacts and creations' in organisational culture we have the symbols, rituals and traditions of the school. If the school culture is to be grasped, let alone articulated, these three areas – symbols, rituals and traditions – will have to be examined. Here we have time for only a brief consideration of them.

Symbols such as school uniforms, mottoes, badges, religious images and school buildings are visible expressions of what the school is about and point to a world of meaning beyond themselves. Other symbols not to be overlooked include school magazines, newsletters and prospectuses, all of which are manifestations of the school's culture and spirit, as well as being descriptions of what the school cherishes and celebrates. Nor must we forget to add to this list school Masses and assemblies – public ceremonies which communicate the meaning and values central to the school's culture. We can classify all these as expressive symbols of the school.[18]

Traditions

The traditions of the school are the manifestations of the core beliefs and values of the school which are handed down from one generation to the next. They are usually couched in stories and myths. In fact, Broms and Gamberg, in *Communication to Self in Organisations and Cultures,* treat of the very concept of culture itself as group values embedded in such stories and myths:

> Symbols and myths are values clothed as a picture, an image ... These images form and maintain culture. The symbols, images, or simply call them group habits, are stored in typical words, picture and actions ... and (are) transmitted from generation to generation.[19]

Traditions, viewed in this light, tell us where the school is coming from, what it is aiming at through its goals, curriculum and heroes, as well as all the processes it uses to achieve its objectives.

What the school is aiming at is probably best encapsulated in its mission statement. This is a very powerful factor in both setting and shaping the school's direction, and its importance is a recurring them in studies of excellence and leadership in schools and organisations generally.[20] The mission statement of a school is best articulated through a process which involves the entire school community examining its core values and vision. The core values are those enduring values which the school cherishes and proclaims. In the case of a Catholic school these will be Gospel values. They should be incorporated in a clear and concise mission statement. The school community involved in drawing up

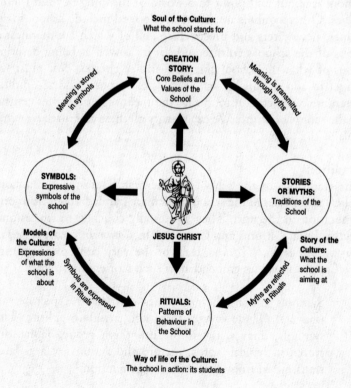

Fig. 3 Flynn's Model

the mission statement, in addition to principal and staff, should include trustees, Board of Management, parents and students.

The symbols, traditions and myths, in a dynamic interaction with each other, give rise to very distinctive patterns of meaning and behaviour among the members of the school community. These patters of behaviour, or rituals, become accepted as the way of life of the school. The rituals are the way 'things are done around here'.[21] They include discipline patterns, class routines and school systems.[22] These tangible aspects and facets of school culture, mentioned above, need to be emphasised in the articulation of ethos, since every culture 'needs its outward and visible signs; only then does it begin to be the uniting influence that it should be.'[23] This level of cultural analysis describes in a general sense how a school or organisation constructs its environment and what we can observe. To analyse why members behave as they do we must look at the values which govern behaviour – the second level of Schein's model.

Levels 2 and 3: Values and underlying assumptions

The second level takes us into the inner circle of Beare's model. As values are difficult to observe directly we often have to infer them by interviewing people, formally and informally, or by analysing the content of documents such as: mission statement; statement of the school's philosophy; enrolment policy; pastoral care programme; co-curricular activities; examination and assessment system; the discipline code. The inferences we make may not be altogether valid since they usually represent accurately only the espoused values of a school culture – what the people say is the reason for their behaviour or what they would ideally like the reasons to be. The real reasons may be hidden (even from the participants themselves): they may be underlying assumptions.

To really understand a culture and to grasp more completely the group's values we need to delve deeper into the underlying assumptions. As Schein observes, 'In a sense all cultural learning reflects someone's original values, their sense of what ought to be, as distinct from what is.'[24] When a group faces a new task, problem or issue, the first solution proposed is based on the convictions about the nature of reality which someone, usually the founder or leader, puts forward. If the solution works and the group has a shared perception of that success, the value gradually starts a process of cognitive transformation into a belief and ultimately, an assumption. As the values, over a period of time and experience, begin to be taken for granted, 'they gradually become beliefs and assumptions and drop out of consciousness, just as habits become unconscious and automatic.'[25]

These assumptions have a quality of absoluteness. They tend to be nonconfrontable and nondebatable. We know that we are dealing with an assumption when we come up against a refusal to discuss something, or when people consider us 'ignorant' for raising some issue. To give a very simple example, the notions that schools should educate, or that medicine should prolong life are assumptions. These underlying assumptions really drive or create values and overt behaviour.

Because of the human need for order and consistency, the basic assumptions gradually come to be co-ordinated into patterns, cultural paradigms – world views – about humankind, nature, reality and activities:

> When a group of people share the same world view, when the paradigms are consistent with each other or are sufficiently homogeneous in their core assumptions, then a common culture emerges.[26]

How can we analyse these cultural paradigms, these patterns of basic assumptions which are the essence of culture? Schein provides us with a tool, a set of logical categories for analysing cultural paradigms. These logical categories are based on the original study of cross-cultural comparisons by Kluckhohn and Strodtbeck[27] and comprise five basic underlying assumptions around which cultural paradigms form. Since these are important in the strategy for cultural analysis we we are outlining we will go into them in some detail.

The five basic assumptions are as follows: Firstly, our relationship to nature and the relationship of the organisation to environment. One needs to assess such things as whether the key members of the organisation view the relationship with the environment as one of dominance, submission, harmony or, alternatively, finding the appropriate niche. Secondly, there is the nature of reality and truth. Here we have the linguistic and behavioural rules that define what is real and what is not, what is a 'fact'; how truth is ultimately to be determined; whether truth is 'revealed' or 'discovered'; the basic concepts of time as linear or cyclical; basic concepts like space as limited or infinite and property as communal or individual. Thirdly, the make-up of human nature: what it means to be 'human' and what attributes are considered intrinsic or ultimate; whether human nature is good, evil or neutral; whether or not human beings are perfectible. Fourthly, the nature of human activity: within the context of the above assumptions about reality, the environment and human nature, what is the 'right' thing for human beings to do? should they be active, passive, self-developmental or fatalistic? what is work and what is play? Fifthly, the nature of human relationships: what is considered the 'right' way for people to relate to one another, to distribute power and love? is life co-operative or competitive, individualistic, group collaborative or communal, based on traditional lineal authority, law or charisma?

When we come to apply these to the school we see that the soul of the culture of the school is its core beliefs and values. In addition to the beliefs and values which members of the school are conscious of, there are many more in their underlying assumptions: beliefs about human nature, the spiritual nature of men and women, education as a development of the whole person, the nature of relationships with other people(community), the environment. At the heart of the Catholic school culture is the person of Christ, the alpha and omega. There is, consequently, at the heart of every Catholic school culture the Christian concept of metanoia: a returning to the basic assumptions of the kingdom of God: Gospel values, faith, social justice and the Church's mission of evangelisation in the world; putting on 'the mind of Christ Jesus'.[28]

These basic assumptions can be surfaced, articulated and brought back to awareness only through a focused inquiry – the efforts of both the insider who makes the unconscious assumptions and the outsider who helps to uncover the assumptions by asking the right questions. Regrettably, many school staff seminars and staff days remain at the first two levels of cultural analysis. The systematic probing of basic assumptions, our third level, would, however, provide a fruitful area for ongoing school staff development.

Any analysis of basic assumptions will inevitably lead us to a core question, what might be termed a crisis of congruence, a tension between espoused values and the lived experience within the school environment. Though lack of space precludes adequate discussion of this area here, we would point out, in passing, that at the heart of every Catholic school is the constant tension between the requirements of academic success and the promotion of moral values. This tension is especially evident in the current climate of intense competitiveness, and one recent writer has called attention to the extent to which such values as honesty, civic-mindedness, tolerance, caring and fellowship are genuinely part of our living culture (basic assumptions) or merely aspirational rhetoric (espoused values).[29]

Ideally, at the level of basic assumptions, a congruent, positive culture influences our lives at two levels: firstly, it defines how we act most of the time. By reducing daily decision-making, culture fosters certainty, promotes freedom, encourages predictability and provides stability in our everyday lives. It structures patterns of thought and perceptions of reality. Secondly, a congruent, positive culture enables people to feel better about what they do, and, consequently, they work more effectively. Communicating a sense of belonging and rootedness gives enriched meaning and purpose to our lives.[30] In contemporary society which, according to Berger,[31] is characterised by 'mental homelessness', people, especially young people, need a context of stable beliefs and values to provide them with the cultural rootedness which all human beings require in order to grow and flourish.[32]

Promotion and development of culture

This brings us to another aspect of the articulation of culture. Rootedness and stability are not to be confused with stagnation and cultural imposition. A brief look at the development of culture ought to bear this out.

Our schools, as open interactive systems with porous boundaries, exist within a broader host culture. Christianity has historically been a central feature of our western and Irish culture. During the present century, however, the advent of radical pluralism has altered matters. It has led to a

> ... global weakening in the holding power of institutions over the individual ... The institutional fabric, whose basic function has always been to provide meaning and stability for the individual, has become incohesive, fragmented and progressively deprived of plausibility.[33]

Cultural messages, other than those coming from home and school, are also being communicated. Our society is changing at an ever-increasing rate and one of the effects of this is that religion is becoming increasingly a personal, private affair. However, this does not mean that people have also become averse to all moral influences, but rather that the young, especially, have grown suspicious of and apathetic towards any body of moral teaching seen to spring from long-established authority.[34] Whatever kind of culture characterises a school it is not something that can be imposed. It is not a one-way process in which pupils, teachers, parents and the wider community conform to some vision of the school imposed from above. Rather, all the agents are partners in a highly interactive process of dialogue – understood as 'a passionate interest in the fraternity and reconciliation of humankind'[35] Students are not only influenced by school culture, but also influence that culture, because culture is a human interplay. In the words of Bates, culture must be constructed and reconstructed constantly:

> Culture, from a cultural studies point of view, is a dialectical process. That is, it is not simply a pre-formed set of beliefs, values, mores and understandings which are passed from one generation to another as if they were objects. Rather, culture is constructed and reconstructed continuously through the efforts of individuals to learn, master and take part in collective life.[36]

The implications of this for leadership are clear: such a culture evolves through shared history and experiences and not through managerial decisions.

Leadership

No paper attempting to outline a strategy which might help towards the articulation of a school culture would be complete without a direct reference to one essential ingredient in the whole enterprise – leadership. Adequate treatment of this topic would, however, require a separate paper and, in the present one, there is space for only a few brief observations on those aspects of leadership which have a direct bearing on our own topic.

Writings on organisational culture, school management and administration constantly refer to the concept of leadership and its central role as a key characteristic of outstanding organisations.[37] Schein, in fact, goes so far as to say that culture and leadership, on closer examination, are two sides of the same coin.[38] A clear distinction between leadership and management also emerges from these writings.

> Management is the use of resources, human and material, to achieve the aims of the school: it is essentially a maintenance function. Leadership is all this and more. It has an additional inspirational dimension: it goes beyond maintenance to transformation. A good staff and a set of rules do not suffice; one also needs a vision and a sense of mission to bond everyone together.[39]

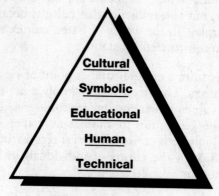

Fig. 4 Sergiovanni's Model

James McGregor Burns (1978) distinguishes between transactional leadership, by which he means getting things done, and transforming leadership, by which he means pointing the way, inspiring and motivating people to make new commitments, and he advocates a combination of both.

Sergiovanni identifies five kinds of leadership force: technical, human, educational, symbolic and cultural. What emerges clearly from this hierarchy of leadership forces, especially the symbolic and cultural forces, is the function of leadership to provide a sense of mission (see fig. 4). This sense of mission or vision can be the driving force of a school. Nothing binds people together more, or is more compelling, than belief in a common cause. Greenfield asserted that 'organisations are built on the unification of people around values.... The business of being a leader is, therefore, the business of being an entrepreneur of values.'[40]

Do schools really matter?

In the 1980s Flynn undertook research into the effect of home and school influences on students' academic performance in public examinations in New South Wales, Australia. The five influences examined were the students' home background (parents' education, socio-economic status and expectations for their children), the formal classroom curriculum, the informal curriculum of the school (ethos, climate and spirit/culture), the religious education curriculum and the quality of school life. He confidently expected that the formal curriculum and the home background would the most decisive factors. But he was surprised to discover that the informal curriculum of the school proved five times more influential than its nearest rivals.[41]

These results are in agreement with Rutter (1979) and dismiss the environmental determinism of the Coleman Report (1966) and of Jencks (1972). The latest research findings strongly support the view that schools *do* make a difference. School culture and ethos do really matter. This is well summed up in the words of Beare *et al*:

What seems to be emerging as a much more powerful factor about the acknowledged best schools is that they have developed a culture, a milieu, environment, atmosphere, a *cultus corporis,* which, in a myriad of ways, influences how well children learn.[42]

These results have a special significance for supporters of the Catholic school, the efficacy of which has been questioned many times in the second half of this century. Flynn's research is significant in that it provides evidence that Catholic schools can be a powerful cultural influence on young people. This is also the contention of Andrew Greeley, who bases his opinion on research on past students of Catholic schools in the US.[43]

Conclusion

In the course of this paper, which looks at an approach to articulating the ethos of a school, the term 'culture' has been chosen as a more encompassing and helpful word for what is usually described as 'ethos'. We have shown that culture is a very elusive concept and must not be oversimplified: it goes beyond slogans and behaviour patterns to basic assumptions, core beliefs and values. We have explained how culture develops and how imposition is foreign to its nature. We have stressed, though not at length, the role of leadership in the development of a school culture. In fact, it could well be that the most important task of a principal is to create the conditions for the development of a positive school culture and manage that culture.

We are well aware that the subject has a vast literature in the fields of anthropology and sociology as well as in the study of business organisations. In this article we have confined ourselves largely to those aspects of culture that pertain to a school. We are also conscious of the fact that the articulation and analysis of school culture may appear new to some teachers and the question will surely arise, is it worthwhile? We would unhesitatingly answer in the affirmative. Lack of insight into culture can leave us vulnerable to forces of evolution and change, which, as we have said above, are very strong at present. Moreover, is it not reasonable to expect that a school, purporting to share its values and vision of life with young people, knows where it is going, what it stands for and what its core values are?

NOTES

1. T. S. Eliot, *Four Quartets* (London: Faber & Faber).
2. C. Hardy and R. Aitken, *Understanding Schools as Organisations* (London: Penguin Books, 1986), p. 79.
3. K. Williams, 'Religious Ethos and State Schools', in *Doctrine & Life*, Vol. 42, no. 9, November 1992, p. 561.
4. C. Anderson, 'The Search for School Climate: A Review of the Research', *Review of Educational Research*, Vol. 52, no. 3, 1982, pp. 368-420.
5. K. Hughes, 'School Ethos and its Relationship with Contemporary Trends in the Secondary School', in B. Spence (ed.), *Aspects of Education*, no. 48, 1993 (Hull: University of Hull), p. 59.
6. T. Peters and R. H. Waterman, *In Search of Excellence* (New York: Harper & Row, 1982), p. 75.
7. M. Jelinek, L. Smirich and P. Hirsch, 'A Code of Many Colours', *Administrative Science Quarterly*, no. 28, September 1983, p. 331.
8. H. Beare, B.J. Caldwell and R.H. Milikan, *Creating an Excellent School* (London and New York: Routledge, 1989), p. 331.
9. M. Rubler, B. Maugham, P. Mortimore and J. Ouston, *Fifteen Thousand Hours – Secondary Schools and Their Effects on Children* (London: Open Books, 1979), pp. 183-4.
10. 'Sailing to Byzantium'.
11. W.M. Abbott (ed.), *Documents of Vatican II* (London: Chapman, 1966), p. 259.
12. H.J. Davis and A. Rasool, 'Values Research and Managerial Behaviour: Implications for Devising Culturally Consistent Managerial Styles', *MIT Review*, Vol. 28, no. 3, 1988.
13. C. Kluckhohn, *Cultural Behaviour* (New York: Free Press, 1962), p. 25.
14. M. McGreil, 'Education and Cultural Development', *Social Studies: Irish Journal of Sociology*, Vol. 1, no. 6, December 1972, p. 668.
15. P. Hogan, 'A Question of Ethos in Schools', *The Furrow*, November 1984.
16. E.H. Schein, *Organizational Culture and Leadership* (San Francisco: Jossey Bass, 1985), p. 3.

17. Ibid.
18. H. Beare *et al,* op. cit., pp. 194-5; M. Flynn, *The Culture of Catholic Schools* (Homebush, NSW: St Pauls, 1993), pp. 43-44.
19. H. Broms and H. Gahmberg, 'Communication to Self in Organizations and Cultures', *Administrative Science Quarterly,* no. 28, September 1983.
20. H. Beare *et al,* op. cit., p. 107; T. Peters and R.H. Waterman, op. cit., p. 260.
21. T.E. Deal and A. Kennedy, *Corporate Cultures: The Rites and Rituals of Corporate Life* (Massachusetts: Addison-Wesley, 1982), p. 4.
22. H. Beare *et al,* op. cit., p. 195; M. Flynn, op. cit., pp. 49-51.
23. C. Handy and R. Aitken, op. cit., p. 79.
24. E.H. Schein, op. cit., p. 15.
25. Ibid., p. 16.
26. H. Beare *et al,* op. cit., p. 18.
27. F.R. Kluckhohn and F.L. Strodtbeck, *Value Orientations* (Evanston: Row Peterson, 1961), quoted in E.H. Schein, 'Coming to a New Awareness of Organizational Culture', in *Sloan Management Review,* MIT, 1984, p. 5.
28. K. Treston, *Transforming Catholic Schools* (Brisbane: Creation Enterprises, 1992), p. 51.
29. K. Williams, op. cit., p. 566.
30. T.E. Deal and A. Kennedy, op. cit., pp. 15-16.
31. P.L. Berger and H. Kellner, *The Homeless Mind* (London: Penguin Books, 1973).
32. Ibid.
33. P.L. Berger and H. Kellner, op. cit., p. 85.
34. P. Hogan, 'Can Goodness be Taught?', *The Furrow,* Vol. 40, no. 2, February 1989, p. 90.
35. P. Hogan, 'A Question of Ethos in Schools', *The Furrow,* Vol. 35, no. 11, November 1984, p. 702.
36. R. Bates, *The Management of Culture and Knowledge* (Melbourne: Dakin University Press, 1986), p. 10.
37. cf. H. Beare *et al;* T.E. Deal and A. Kennedy; C. Handy and R. Aitken; T. Peters and R.H. Waterman; E.H. Schein, op. cit.
38. E.H. Schein, op. cit., p. 2.

39. C. Handy and R. Aitken, op. cit., p. 83.
40. T.B. Greenfield, 'Leaders and Schools: Willfulness and Non-Natural Order in Organizations', in T.J. Sergiovanni and J.E. Corbally (eds.), *Leadership and Culture* (Chicago: University of Chicago Press, 1986), p. 166.
41. M. Flynn, *The Culture of Catholic Schools* (New South Wales: St Paul's, Homebush, 1993), p. 5.
42. H. Beare *et al,* op. cit., p. 18.

HELPING PARENTS HELP THEIR CHILDREN DURING SCHOOLING

Ruth Brennock

Edmund Rice was himself a parent and his followers initiated the structures that promoted the involvement of parents in schools in Ireland in the early 1970s. This was effected by the formation of parent councils in schools. These act as a support for the schools and help to bond parents together to work effectively for the school and in any other area that would contribute to the education and development of their children. In order to carry out this task, formation work was undertaken with parents whenever possible. The movement eventually culminated in the formation of the National Parents' Council (NPC) in 1985, by the then Minister for Education, Gemma Hussey.

The National Parents' Council Post-Primary (NPCpp) is a Council of Councils – an umbrella organisation of eight constituent bodies, all of which are themselves organised at national level. This organisation has a federal structure and seeks to work by consensus as much as possible.

NPC mission statement

Our NPC mission statement is both instructive and prescriptive.

> The National Parents' Council (NPC), in a spirit of unity and caring, aims to coordinate the energy and ideas of its constituent bodies to promote the spiritual, intellectual, physical, social and psychological education of the nation's children. To this end, NPC enables the further education and personal development of parents to foster the growth of children as responsible adults.

Implicit in this mission statement is our understanding not only of education but also of the role of parents in education. I am here including schooling as part of what I regard as the larger and wider concept of education. We believe that education is fundamentally a process and only secondarily a system of structures. This process begins at the moment of birth and blossoms into the wisdom of mature age. It is lifelong and continuing – from cradle to grave.

Education is a process whereby persons come to maturity and wholeness, integrating the various dimensions of human life: the spiritual, intellectual, physical, social and psychological potentialities of the human person. We parents believe that this process involves not only the acquisition of a knowledge base and skills for living, but also entails growth in all the dimensions of the human personality, especially in those moral and emotional sensitivities which make possible our common life as a human family (NPC Green Paper Submission).

How can parents help and enhance this process we call education? A brief look at the second part of the NPC mission statement gives hints as to how this may be accomplished. A good way to start is with the basic questions: Why should it be done? How should it be done? Where should it be done?

These are exciting times of change in education. At last we parents are being given our rightful place as partners in the system, with all the challenges this entails. We can be justly proud of an education system that served us well. Now that we face into a changing world we must strive to integrate what is best from the past with the changes of the future. But we feel these changes should be evolutionary rather than revolutionary. It is a tribute to the value that parents, teachers and pupils place on education that such excellence occurs, even in spite of the crippling cut-backs of recent years. We parents played no mean part in the attainment of this excellence by raising up to 25 per cent of the operational expenditure of schools to meet shortfalls and to provide what we regard as essentials for our schools. Perhaps even more significant was our personal contribution in lending our personal and professional skills, to say nothing of our moral support.

The role of the parent has changed radically over the past twenty years as, indeed, has that of the school and the teacher. The complexities of modern life, the erosion of the extended family support system, the emergence of forms of family different from the traditional two-parent unit, and the urban drift are some of the factors that have altered the shape and structure of society. New and more meaningful ways of meeting family needs must now be examined.

To help parents help their children get the most out of schooling, it is essential that they play their role as partners in the education system. The Green Paper was eloquent on parent partnership, but strangely silent about how this should be accomplished. To enable parents take their place as partners we need the empowerment of knowledge and training. There is some training available in this area, but it is fragmented, uncoordinated and very limited. It could be argued that parenting is something that evolves naturally, part of the human condition. This view, although having a certain validity, overlooks the changing nature of our society today and the speed at which changes are occurring. The traditional supports of the past are fading away, so the parent and the family need new back-up in the complex and demanding world of education today.

The emerging concept of the school as a system of partners in which parents, teachers and trustees share a common vision, a system where all these play an interlinking part and support each other, a system whereby parents and teachers support each other in dealing with the problems of society now appearing in the classroom, requires that each group be equipped to play its role. A very effective method is the provision of training programmes delivered by parents themselves in the school, using the parent association or council as a forum for delivery.

Parent education programmes are needed to address two distinct but related areas. The first would provide training for the parent involved at the institutional level, whether this be on a board of management, parent council or any other body involved in education.

It needs to include skills as well as information-based modules: skills needed to participate in boards of management, to set up parents' councils, to run meetings, draw up budgets, make out agendas and so on. It needs to include information on how the education system works, on the meaning of specialised terminology, on policy issues, curriculum, resourcing, history and psychology of the system, and other areas as required.

The second would provide programmes that would respond to the needs of parents in the area of personal development and parenting skills to help us function effectively as educators of our own children and thus draw forth all their potential for growth in love and affirmation as whole people. This would also provide us with continuing education for ourselves, and would include the following:

Personal development
Confidence-building
Intra-family relational skills
Understanding family systems
Awareness of one's relationship to others, to the world of leisure
    and culture
Development of self-esteem
Awareness of the significance and role of self

Skills
Listening and Communication
Conflict resolution
Stress control
Agreed loving discipline

Any parent training programme needs to respond to the life-cycle needs of parents, from those of new parents right through life's journey. Such programmes must at all times be non-intrusive and respectful of the experiences of parents themselves. They must respond to the identified needs of the parents, based on a knowledge of what we ourselves want, not what others might think we need.

We parents harbour great expertise within ourselves. Any parent who has reared a child from birth to adulthood has a wealth of wisdom and knowledge to share. Parents at the various life-cycle stages have much to offer, and peer parents can support each other. A framework is needed to draw out all this expertise to help and support each other in the task of parenting today.

This must be a basic function of any parenting programme. The trainers themselves could be parents, after going through an appropriate course. In this way parents pool and share their expertise and relate more meaningfully to each other; although we are 'experts' ourselves, we often lack the self-confidence to acknowledge our own giftedness. The ideal venue is the school and the ideal setting the parent association or council.

The kind of programme envisaged would be beyond the meagre resources of the NPC and its constituent bodies. It needs funding either at Government or EU level. An investment in such a training programme would be cost-effective in socio-economic terms. This is given recognition in the Programme for Competitiveness and Work. Programmes like this act as powerful agents in the reduction of disadvantage and the development of parenting skills, thus improving the quality of family life and, thereby, enhancing society. As parents assist in the development of children as whole, well-rounded, responsible citizens, the despair and low self-esteem that cause the drift into crime, drug and alcohol abuse, and the many other ills bedevilling society would be addressed. It is to be hoped that a result would be less demand on the social services. Such programmes will inevitably enrich society.

The National Parents' Council, post-primary and primary divisions, collaborated on such a programme and produced the training and education programme *Parents in Partnership*. The Department of Education was approached for funding, but to no avail. The programme was then submitted to the European Commission, where we are trying to get it funded as a pilot for Europe. In the meantime, we will draw up the programme and try to get funding from the Department for a 'pilot of the pilot', and get started as soon as possible.

Facing the future

In the meantime reality must be faced and what can be done now must be explored. How does what is happening in education fit in with the mission statement? Despite the best efforts it leaves much to be desired. This is no reflection on schools or teaching but on the way in which education has been subverted in recent years by allowing pressures that diminish education as a process to go unchecked, for example the points race; high pupil/teacher ratios; inadequate guidance counselling; limited psychological services.

An open and honest look must be taken at the present system. The rat race for points is inimical to the true meaning of education. It is destructive of that joyful journey which should characterise education and replaces it with the narrow competitive goal of X number of points, thereby pushing out some of the vitally important dimensions of the education of the whole person. It can engender a spirit of ruthless competitiveness and is hardly conducive to idealism, compassion and caring. We parents need to pause and reflect on what can happen to the young human psyche in this frantic scramble for third-level places.

Increased competitiveness and the pressure for points are perhaps the most damaging changes to have taken place in schools over the years. They go a long way towards robbing young people of the freedom of spirit which genuine education should foster. It is sad that the measure of the merit of a young student is the number of points gained in an examination.

The pressures experienced in senior cycle affect junior cycle and press on down to primary level, where there can be pressure to teach for secondary entrance or grading exams, thus, yet again, limiting time for developmental work. This has even found its way, in some instances, to pre- and play school, where tiny children get homework, and are taught to read and write during time which should be used for socialisation, development of motor skills, co-ordination and play. The span of childhood is sadly getting shorter and shorter as children are hothoused into adulthood. We parents can contribute to all of this in our efforts to give our children a good start. We are now learning that in many cases our goals for our children can be too narrowly focused and our expectations unrealistic. There is now the fear that exam results and career achievement may be perceived as the measure of self-worth.

To help parents help their children get the most out of schooling, a sense of the enjoyment of the process of learning needs to be highlighted, so that we can encourage our children to focus on education as a joyful journey of discovery and intellectual challenge, and not be gripped by fear regarding the outcome. When the educational journey is one of joy and discovery the outcome generally takes care of itself.

We can get involved with the school by joining the parents' association and using it as a forum for information and the sharing of experiences. The best help, advice and support I have received has been from fellow parents, particularly those whose children were a little older than mine. If there is no association we can approach the principal to help us set up one.

Those of us who are lucky enough to have that enlightened initiative, the Home/School/Community Liaison Scheme in our school should avail of it to the full.

The NPC can provide training for parents. A simple training course for leaders would enable many parents to run training sessions. Tasks would include informing parents of policy and curricular developments through parent council meetings, workshops, discussion and presentations.

Co-operation between parents and teachers

There must be an ongoing process to explore new ways of co-operation between parents and teachers. This requires new initiatives to promote greater bonding between parents and teachers by means of open and honest communication and understanding. We can also encourage school principals to promote the concept of the 'welcoming school'.

Research shows that home/school partnership has a positive influence on the children's academic achievement levels, sense of well-being, attitudes to school and development in wholeness. In addition, the research suggests that home/school partnership can reduce the level of failure and counteract the effects of disadvantage. The evidence also shows that participation in home/school partnership can be achieved by all parents, irrespective of social background or educational achievement.

Close collaboration between school and home gives a strong message to the child. It has a tremendous bearing on attitudes and demonstrates the interlinking of the two systems as a natural progression. It fosters the ideal of the school as an extension of the home. It is therefore important to hold parent council meetings in the school, not at the local hotel or hall, and to host all council social and fundraising functions there also.

What can we do as parents to help our children in practical ways?

We must listen actively to our children. Quite often the problem expressed is not the real, underlying problem, so we should listen without interruption, then reflect back what we hear. This will evoke a further response. Our children feel valued when this happens. It raises confidence and self-esteem. True self-esteem helps a young person acknowledge his or her own strengths, gifts and weaknesses. We can reflect on how we affirm the strengths and gifts and give positive messages to enable the child to strengthen his or her weaknesses. A child with a proper sense of self-esteem is very open to travelling that road of joyful discovery and having a love of learning. That pupil is well-disposed to getting the most out of schooling.

Effective listening and open communication facilities, discussion and sharing between parent and child can make the child feel respected. This sharing can help identify any anxieties or worries that may be troubling him or her. We can help our children to explore their feelings, although this is not because any feelings they may have should guide their lives. Feelings are neither right nor wrong, but how they are acted out or dealt with may be. Feelings that we are not even aware of can influence decisions without our even knowing it. Becoming aware of feelings is vital in learning how to deal with them rationally and thereby helps children to act out of reason and personal values.

Self-esteem and responsibility

A child who has fears can then identify where those fears are coming from and thus be helped to deal with them. This has a positive influence on schooling. The cultivation of self-esteem and responsibility are vital elements in our children's development and hence, also, in schooling.

The teen years are both exciting and difficult – facing into the adult world, experiencing physical, sexual and emotional change and growth. Growing towards and discovering freedom is challenging and sometimes fearful and confusing. It is not easy for parents, either. We are learning to let go, to watch our children make their own mistakes and learn from them. We have few set rules or formulas to fall back on. All of us are different and get through as best we can. Perhaps we too learn from our mistakes, but the bottom line is that our children need to experience our love, support and affirmation in tangible ways. They, in common with all humans, need the assurance that they are lovable and loving, no matter what mistakes they make or what their performance level in school is. Our affirmation is crucial to the development of self-esteem. Fostering self-esteem, good listening and communication is central to assisting our young people grow into responsibility. A confident, responsible, pupil will get his or her best out of schooling.

Positive discipline

Discipline, problem-solving and addressing family conflict are important areas, not only in relation to the child's performance and development at school, but also in the creation of a loving and supportive ethos in the home.

Discipline needs to have connotations of following the right way, in keeping with the meaning of the word, disciple. Deviations from this will bring certain consequences, not punishment, as such, but an opportunity of learning the better way from the consequences. We can involve our children in decision-making about rules and limits that are reasonable, simple and liveable for all. We need to establish our own non-negotiable ground rules at the beginning, and to have logical reasons for and explanations of them. The purpose of rules and limits should be to hold adolescents responsible for their behaviour. Rules and limits should also be open to alteration in response to a changing situation. Thus, the greater their personal growth, the more young people should be encouraged to exercise their independence.

Discipline in the home gives a sense of security and love to our children. It is a very tangible means of expressing our care for their well-being. It fosters self-discipline, is carried into all areas of life, especially schooling, when the pressure is on and a commitment is called for during the exam years. During these exam years we can help parents to help pupils by helping parents to see the value of balance in life-style and the importance of healthy living. We can encourage our children to incorporate relaxation, sport and reflection into their daily timetables.

We can also seek advice from the school about the most effective study methods and help implement these in a flexible way. The pastoral care team has special skills in this area. We parents praise the successful child, and rightly so, when success crowns endeavour, but it is even more important to praise the effort involved, at all times, especially for those who give of their best and experience difficulty in achieving the desired result.

We can take extra care to promote a calm, peaceful atmosphere in the home, we can be flexible and accommodating regarding any passing idiosyncrasies, such as meals at midnight, unorthodox sleeping patterns and many other such activities.

There are homes which may be suffering a degree of dysfunction for various reasons, some may be long-term, others transient. How can parents help here in a respectful, non-intrusive way?

The parents' council as a resource

A parents' council can help. Practical assistance can be given by council members, if appropriate and acceptable to the distressed family.

The council, with the blessing of management, could supervise study in the school for those students taking public examinations. This would benefit all students, especially those where the home environment lacks space and quiet.

Management can also play its part in empowering parents in making the 'welcoming school' a reality, by taking parents as they are, by supporting any initiatives for training and by seeking parents' support in any areas where it can be given for the good of the school.

There are initiatives in place in community and comprehensive schools where parent/teacher liaison committees are in place to develop understanding, partnership and co-operation, to exchange views and inform parents.

Open and honest communication is needed between parents

and teachers, together with an acknowledgement of any anxieties and fears on either side, and the good will to address these.

The professionalism of teachers must at all times be respected, as must the right of parents to be actively involved in their children's education. As a child spends less than 16 per cent of his or her time in school, there is a need for informed parents to foster the informal education process.

We want our Christian schools to give priority to the education of their pupils in a living faith, whereby they can grow to appreciate the life and mission of Jesus, with a view to working for peace and justice in our society.

As Lubbock says, 'The important thing is not so much that every child should be taught, but that every child be given the wish to learn'.

REFERENCES

National Parents' Council Submission to the Green Paper, *Education for a Changing World.*

National Parents' Council Submission to the National Education Convention.

Federation of Christian Brothers' Secondary Schools Submission to the Green Paper.

Donal Leader, *Parent Education: The Task and Challenge,* Marino Institute of Education, 1993.

F. Dorr, *An Introduction to Social and Health Education,* Cork Social and Health Education Office.

National Parents' Council, *Parents as Partners.*

THE GOSPEL SCHOOL

F.J. Steele

In his interpretative summary of the life and abiding significance of Edmund Rice, Cardinal Daly* was at pains to emphasise the centrality of the spiritual in the life, thought and work of the Founder. The heart of Edmund was fixed on the Kingdom of God and the inspiration and support for all that he accomplished derived, not from any human source, however exalted, but from faith in Christ Jesus and in the Good News of the Kingdom. For us who seek in the sesquicentenary of his death to isolate, appreciate and celebrate the peculiar giftedness in Christ of Edmund Rice, it is imperative to see him, his life and his work, as rooted in the Gospel and, ultimately, intelligible and explicable only *sub specie aeternitatis.* Christ makes sense of Edmund and we who would, in whatever fashion, walk in his steps must know, before and above all else, that his is the way of Christ, that the *sequela Edmundi* is itself always and everywhere a *sequela Christi.* True of all aspects of fellowship with Edmund, this is especially true of that aspect of fellowship with him which involves us in the Christian education of youth and, in this particular regard, it may be both opportune and appropriate that, one hundred and fifty years after his death, on the very eve of the Third Millennium, in a time of unprecedented development for the People of God and the family of Edmund, we take our bearings, and ponder again the possible consequences of accepting the Lord Jesus Christ as the Alpha and the Omega, the centre and the circumference, as it were, of all education in the light of the Gospel and for the sake of the Kingdom.

Christ is 'the first-born of all creation ... the beginning, the first-born from the dead' (Col 1:15.18). He is the Second Adam (cf. Rom 5:4), the Heavenly Man (cf. I Cor 15:42-52), the prog-

---

*This article is the revised text of a response by Dr Steele to the feature address by Cardinal Cahal B. Daly at the Conference on Education and the Family at UCC on 28 May 1994. A revised version of Cardinal Daly's address is reproduced at p. 8ff. of this volume.

enitor and the pattern of humanity redeemed and recreated. He is 'the image of the invisible God' (Col 1:15), through, with and in whom, in the power of the Spirit, is restored the image and likeness of God, in which humanity was formed by a gracious, merciful and faithful Creator (cf. Gen 1:26-27), which, in its idolatrous pursuit of 'graven images' (cf. Ex 20:4-6), humanity itself distorts and caricatures, but which, human weakness, blindness and stubborness notwithstanding, is still and always the only sure foundation and vindication of human dignity, equality and, in the end, death-transcending destiny. Christ is, indeed, 'the way, and the truth, and the life' (Jn 14:6), the origin and the end, the paradigm, the explication, the means to, and the measure of humanity. Christ, therefore, is "that living stone, rejected by men but in God's sight chosen and precious' (I Pet 2:4), 'the head of the corner' (I Pet 2:7), the keystone, the bonding stone, the only sure bedrock of all education, and of all educational initiatives and institutes, projects and programmes, that espouse the values of the Gospel and claim the designation of Christian.

This being the case, it would, I think, be useful, enlightening and challenging to consider the ethical core of Catholic schooling, not by means of a ratiocinative discourse on the Christian formation of youth, but by means of that which monastic tradition would designate a *ruminatio,* a meditative, prayerful 'digestion', as it were, of words and images of Scripture meant, in this instance, to help us address and comprehend the inner and enduring reality of that which might be termed the Christ School, the Gospel School, the place and community of teaching and learning where Edmund Rice and Nano Nagle and the Lord himself might be at home.

Because it would be about Christ, the Gospel School would be, primarily, fundamentally, definitively, not about ideas or disciplines or courses, but about people, and not about ideal people or about perfect people or about holy people, but about these people, as they are, right here and right now. The Gospel School would be, not about some people, but about all people, about the son who strayed and about the son who stayed (Lk 15:11-32), about 'the people of the land', about 'these little ones' (cf. Mt 18:6). It would be open, inclusive and, if biased at all, would –

like Christ himself and like Edmund after him – be biased towards the poor, the powerless, the marginalised, the 'lost'.

The Gospel School would regard and accept people in the wholeness and in the complexity in which they are created. Such a school would see its fundamental and definitive role as the formation, not of artists or of scientists, not of producers or of consumers, not even of citizens, but, primarily, of people, of people gifted by God and obligated by this giftedness to become, in Christ, their own most authentic selves, at the service of God and of their neighbour. This school would educate people even as it taught subjects and would, in so doing, mould and tutor both the questing mind and the restless heart and would resist all that reduced and reified the human person by identifying humanity with anything partial, anything incomplete, anything less than the fullness of personhood in which each is made by a loving God whose intent it is 'that they may have life, and have it abundantly' (Jn 10:10).

In such a school there would be constant need for a vision of humanity which saw Christ in everyone. There would be need for the eyes of a Simeon (cf. Lk 2:22-35), of an Anna (cf. Lk 2:36-38), to discern the presence of the Lord in the midst of crowds and confusion. There would be need, indeed, for an experience of something akin to 'transfiguration', that in the face of each committed to our care we might detect the bright reflection of the Fatherhood of God; that we might listen, not to the sound of self, not even to the sound of self doing good, but to that which the Lord would say to us both of divinity and of humanity in each and in all of his 'beloved' (cf., e.g., Mt 17:1-8). There would be need, besides, in the Gospel School for an awareness of the 'courtesy' of God who, when met upon the way, does indeed put to us that which may transform our understanding of reality, but who will never impose himself upon us, who will always, in respect for our freedom, make as if to go on (cf. Lk 24:13-35).

Because it will be about Christ and, thus, about people, the Gospel School will be about community. It will be about identification and integration by, and before, the Lord. The people who constitute the community of teaching and learning that is the school are never together as a result of blind chance. It is always the providence of God that brings together, and holds together, pupils, parents and staff in any school. The Gospel School, however, is a kind and mode of assembly of God's holy people and, for this reason, alongside 'the domestic church', 'the church of the home', we may set 'the scholastic church', 'the church of the school', the gathering and communion in Christ of those whom the Father has called to be the means and the occasion of witness and worship in the ever-to-be-evangelised new-found-land of youth. In such a Spirit-made community, there can, of course, be no rightful place either for a 'them' or for an 'us'. In the Gospel School, there is but one Rabbi, one Father, one Master (cf. Mt 23:8-10). All are 'brothers' (cf. Mt 23:8), all are co-disciples, and, as in all 'churches', as in all assemblies gathered in Christ, so in the school that is gathered in Christ, authority is indeed given, but is given, not for self or for power, but for others and for service (cf. Jn 13:1-20).

Because all of this is 'scandalous', 'a stumbling block to Jews and folly to Gentiles' (I Cor 1:23), we who would be and become the Gospel School must 'not be conformed to the world' (Rm 12:2). We must 'repent, and believe in the gospel' (Mk 1:15). We must, in fact, be 'transformed by the renewing of [our] minds (cf. Rom 12:2) until we have in us 'that mind ... which was in Christ Jesus' (Ph 2:5), until we are converted and see things as God sees them and live our entire lives accordingly. This process of metanoia must involve and envelop, not just ourselves, but the communities of learning and of teaching of which we are part. The Gospel School is, in one sense, never established but always a-founding, because, day in, day out, it is constantly seeking and becoming its own most authentic reality in the depths of the reality of Christ. As with the Kingdom, so with the Gospel School, it is always a matter of 'already' and 'not yet', always a matter of both 'event' and 'process', always a matter of both 'being' and 'becoming', until, in the fullness of time, it is 'restored' in Christ and Christ is all in all.

The Gospel School, therefore, will also be the Pilgrim School, still in *via*, not yet in *patria*, ever Christian but always in need of Christianisation, never content with what it is but unceasingly becoming what it is meant to be. The Gospel School will be a *peregrinus,* a 'pilgrim', an 'exile', a 'resident alien'. It will be part of the things that are in time yet faithful witness to the things that matter in eternity. This, precisely, will be the 'crisis', the occasion of temptation, decision, judgement, for the Gospel School in its often all too earthly, mundane and, even, secular pilgrimage – to balance the urgent claims of the temporal against the ineluctable demands of the eternal; to be, and to teach others to be, both 'resident' and 'alien', ready for life here and fit for life hereafter, in the world but not of the world, using the world as though they used it not (cf. I Cor 7:31); totally, positively, generously open to the exigencies and complexities of human life in the here and now and still with heart and mind fixed on the *unum necessarium* (cf. Lk 10:42).

To endure and transcend the condition of its pilgrimage, the Gospel School must be, besides, the Faith School. The circumstances of such a school will not differ from those of any other and, even in the Christ School, the incarnation of the Good News must needs occur in the world as it is and in a humanity which is itself weak, misguided, sinful, prey to all that is anti-Gospel, anti-Christian, as ready as not to counter and contradict in deed that which it proclaims in word. The points race, the ratrace, the joys and fears, the wear and tear of everyday experience, constitute the inescapable context of this process of pilgrimage and, without the insight of a Jacob – that insight which, even in the face of the material at its most irreducible and at its most inflexible, can still recognise the presence of the Lord, can still confess 'This is none other than the house of God, and this is the gate of heaven' (Gn 28:17) – that which would and should be the Gospel School will be easily and inextricably enmeshed in the soul-engrossing solicitude of the day until, between it and its wholly secular counterpart, there is no distinction evident to either God or humankind.

The Gospel School, of course, will not be absorbed in itself and in the matter of its own identity and distinctiveness. It will be other-oriented, concerned with and for the service of God and the neighbour. It will seek '...to preach good news to the poor ...to proclaim release to the captives and recovering of sight to the blind, to set at liberty those who are oppressed, to proclaim the acceptable year of the Lord' (Lk 4:18-19'. It will be at the service of truth, of that truth which, because it is grounded and vindicated in the absolute reality of 'I am who I am' (Ex 3:14), offers to humanity liberation from the threat of ultimate unreality, unrealisation, annihilation (cf. Jn 8:32). In the Gospel School, education will be an Exodus, a going up to the fullness of life (cf. Jn 10:10), an enfranchisement in respect of human culture, an empowerment in respect of all that produces and protects the dignity of the children of the God and Father of the Lord Jesus Christ.

Again, it is necessary to emphasise that the task of the Gospel School is not one that can be discharged in isolation, splendid or otherwise, from 'the bulks of actual things'. The desert is seldom a real option for the Gospel School. The place of the served must always be the location of the service and it is in doing those things that we are obliged to do that we, like Peter and Andrew, James and John (cf. Mk 1:16-20), are, as it were, put in the way of hearing the call of Christ. Like all education, education for the sake of the Gospel implicates us in humanity at its most human, fractious, cross-grained, contrary. Like all education, education for the sake of the Gospel involves us in the world at its most worldly where ambition and emulation are the natural motors of progress and where competition is inculcated even as co-operation is celebrated. In such circumstances, in, and, more importantly for, these changing and challenging times, to find words and images for expressing Edmund, to find, thereafter, ways and means of being Edmund, is a necessary, even an urgent, task. Its conduct amongst all who constitute the *familia Edmundi* may, perhaps, turn out to be the single, most important manifestation of the continued presence and power amongst the People of God of the giftedness in Christ of Edmund Ignatius Rice.

BIOGRAPHICAL NOTE ON VENERABLE EDMUND RICE

J. Matthew Feheney FPM

Edmund Rice, founder of both the Presentation and Christian Brothers, was born in Callan, Co. Kilkenny, on 1 June 1762. He came from a large family of seven boys. He also had two step-sisters, children of his mother by a previous marriage. His father was a farmer with almost two hundred acres of land, leased from a local Protestant landlord, Lord Desart. In comparison with the majority of Irish Catholics of the period, his family were considered 'well-off'.

Education

In keeping with the practice of the time, Edmund was taught his prayers and the basics of his religion by his mother at home. At the age of seven he began to attend a local 'hedge' school in Callan. Since schools operated by Catholics were illegal, the 'hedge' schools had a precarious existence. Though generally located in little thatched houses, called cabins, both pupils and teacher might, at any moment, have to disappear and seek refuge in the fields and woods if the local magistrate, accompanied by his yeomanry, appeared in the area. At that time most of the local landlords were invested with the power of magistrates. In fairness, it must be said that quite a few of the gentry did not agree with the harsh penal laws against Catholics, especially those which prevented their children receiving an education. But as they were part of the ruling class, they felt that they had to be seen to uphold the law. And the law stated specifically that no Catholic could operate a school.

The deplorable physical amenities of the 'hedge' school did not, however, prevent Edmund from quickly mastering the 'three R's', and, at the age of fifteen, he moved on to a more advanced school in Kilkenny, operated by a Mr White, a Catholic. Here the curriculum included 'Mathematics, Latin, Greek, French, Grammar, Book-keeping, Globes, Maps, Drawing, Music and

Fencing'. We do not know whether Edmund took all these subjects, but, being a conscientious young man, he probably took most of them. At any rate we know that he excelled at mathematics and book-keeping. Moreover, the progress he was making in his studies, allied to his natural courtesy and good manners, attracted the attention of his uncle, Michael Rice, a successful merchant and ship's chandler in Waterford.

Into business

Edmund's uncle, Michael, was so impressed with his nephew that he invited him to join him as an apprentice in his business. With the full approval of his parents, Edmund accepted this generous invitation and, before long, he was his uncle's right-hand assistant. Though Michael Rice had two sons of his own, neither was interested in their father's business. His nephew, Edmund, on the other hand, had a great flair for it: he was quick at figures, he was a good organiser and he got on well with people. After a few years it became obvious to Uncle Michael that his nephew was the most suitable person to succeed him in charge of the business and, when he died, it was no surprise to anyone that Edmund inherited it. A bright future stretched ahead of him: though not yet thirty years of age, he already owned a flourishing business. Edmund's knowledge of business and legal affairs and his prudence and sound judgment were beginning to be recognised and appreciated by his growing circle of friends. In 1787 his own father, Robert Rice, got him to draw up his will and made him executor of it, even though Edmund was then only twenty-five years of age and was only the fourth son in the family. This was just one of the many instances where people showed their confidence in his skill and integrity. As the years went by, he would be called on by many people to execute their wills, to invest their money and to make legal representations on their behalf.

Marriage and tragedy

At the age of twenty-three, Edmund married a young woman, thought to be named Mary Elliott, the daughter of a well-to-do neighbour. Little is known for certain about her, though tradition says that she was outgoing and vivacious with a great love of horse-riding. About a year after the marriage she died suddenly. Some say her death came as a result of a fall from a horse while out riding, others from a fever. She was pregnant at the time and, before she died, she gave birth to a baby girl, also named Mary, who seems to have been handicapped.

Edmund's world seemed to collapse about him: in one cruel blow fate deprived him of his much-loved wife and gave him instead a handicapped daughter.

Prayer and the Bible

Though initially overcome by grief, he soon accepted with resignation the cross laid on him by a Providence he firmly believed to be compassionate and loving. It brought home to him the transient nature of human joy and the need to look beyond this life for lasting happiness. Though his business flourished under his wise and painstaking management, he began to give more attention to his spiritual life. He acquired his own copy of the Bible and began to read it daily. He underlined texts which made a deep impression on him and returned to these again and again. Always a practical man, he paid special attention to what the Bible had to say about honesty in business affairs. The following are some of the texts found underlined in Edmund's bible.

> If you lend money to any of my people, to any poor man among you, you must not play the usurer with him: you must not demand interest from him. (Ex 22:25)

> Oppress the poor and you enrich him, give to the rich and you make him poor. (Prov 22:16)

> Repent, renounce all your sins, avoid all occasions of sin! Shake off all the sins you have committed against me, and make yourselves a new heart and a new spirit! (Ex 18:31)

> Give to anyone who asks, and if anyone wants to borrow, do not turn away. (Mt 5:42).

> Instead, love your enemies and do good, and lend without any hope of return. You will have a great reward, and you

will be sons of the Most High, for he himself is kind to the ungrateful and the wicked. (Lk 6:35)

Charitable works

Edmund took an active part in the charitable work of his adopted city of Waterford. When two young Connolly girls suddenly became orphans, Edmund had them reared and educated at his own expense. When the Gaelic poet, Tagh Gaelach O'Sullivan, underwent a religious conversion and wished to publish a book of religious poems in a Pious Miscellany, Edmund was one of those who subscribed to the publication of the volume. He was also a signatory to a petition to King George III protesting against the wording of the Oath of Allegiance which Catholics found offensive. This petition was forwarded to His Majesty by a committee of the people of Waterford in 1792 and was one of the events that helped to prepare the climate for the Relief Act of 1793. But one of his most enduring and enlightened actions was to negotiate a lease for the site of Presentation Convent, Waterford, on 1 June 1799. This was Edmund's first encounter with the spiritual daughters of Nano Nagle, a woman he greatly admired and whose example he was eventually to emulate.

Soon after they were established in Waterford, the Presentation Sisters had to call on Edmund Rice again for advice about their financial affairs. Edmund invested their small capital so as to give the best possible dividend. In return, the Sisters loaned him a copy of their Rule, and he studied it with more than casual curiosity.

Meantime, Edmund had begun to attend daily Mass and to read religious books. In the year 1794 he and some friends founded a society for visiting the sick and lonely as well as helping them out financially. As this work expanded it brought him into contact with the poor people living in the slums of Waterford. He was especially touched by the sight of many young boys who were not attending school and were growing up, not only ignorant of their religion, but also unable to read or write and without discipline or restraint of any kind. Today, we might call them juvenile delinquents. The only free schools were Protestant and the teachers in those felt they were entitled to proselytise any

Catholic pupils who attended. True, there were some small private Catholic schools but they charged fees and were intended for the children of more prosperous Catholics. Free primary education, as we know it today, was as yet unheard of in Ireland.

Ministry to poor boys

Very soon Edmund, though engaged in business during the day, began a ministry of his own in the evenings. When he finished work he would open up his own house to poor boys, giving them meals and teaching them their prayers and catechism. He also gave lessons in reading and writing to those boys who were interested. When he saw the tattered clothes of the boys Edmund's business training and flair came to the rescue: he purchased a bale of cloth, hired a tailor and had him make suits for the boys. Shoes were his next venture: he purchased the leather in bulk and hired a shoemaker to make shoes for the boys.

As the number of boys increased, Edmund looked around for larger premises. He purchased a building, formerly used as a stable, with good stone walls, and made the ground floor into a classroom, while upstairs he made space for the tailor and shoemaker. This was Edmund Rice's first school. It provided what the pupils wanted: clothing, shoes and education. But soon he became aware of the fact that the boys were sometimes hungry. So his next initiative was a bakery. Now, in addition to the other things, the boys could be sure of a good meal.

Though Edmund was the first teacher of these boys, as the tailor's shop, the shoemaker's shop and the bakery developed, he had less time for teaching so he looked around for helpers and found some. It was comparatively easy to find a tailor, a shoemaker and a baker, but teachers proved more difficult, not least because the boys were very rough and difficult to control. The teachers whom he initially engaged gave up in frustration and departed and, for a while, the future of the project seemed in danger. But Edmund put his trust in Providence and, when things things seemed hopeless, two young men arrived from his native Callan offering their services and asking to join him in his work. These first companions attracted others and Edmund's school prospered and grew.

Religious congregation

Meantime, however, he began to feel the call to give up his business and devote himself fulltime to the work of educating poor boys. The ecclesiastical rules of the day demanded that any religious group requiring approval from Rome had to live a monastic life and wear religious habit. Inspired by the example of Nano Nagle, Edmund attended the first Mass celebrated in the new Presentation Convent Waterford on the Feast of St Joseph, 19 March 1801. One year later, in 1802, he took the historic decision to found a small community of Brothers of the Presentation. He had studied the Presentaton Rule of the religious sisters of Nano Nagle and had come to the conclusion that what they had done for poor girls, God was calling him and his companions to do for poor boys.

Much suffering

Edmund's decision to found a religious congregation ensured that there would be a steady stream of young men joining him to continue his work. Initially the group was called the Society of the Presentation, the members being popularly known as the Monks of the Presentation and, also, as the Gentlemen of the Presentation. In 1803 Edmund built a new monastery and school in Ballybricken, outside the walls of the city of Waterford, and called it Mount Sion. Here he and his companions made vows of chastity, poverty and obedience in 1808, and began to wear a black habit – indoors only in deference to the Protestant susceptibilities of the ruling establishment.

As the number of volunteers joining Edmund increased, he acceded to requests from priests and Bishops in other towns and dioceses to open schools. Soon there was a network of them: Carrick-on-Suir (1806), Dungarvan (1807), Cork (1811), Dublin (1812), Limerick (1816), Thurles (1816) Preston (1825).

Edmund encountered many difficulties in the second half of his life: the religious congregation he founded later split in two, one group becoming known as the Christian Brothers, while the other retained the Presentation name and are, today, known as Presentation Brothers; certain members of the clergy and some bishops opposed him, while some brothers in his own congregation suspected, misunderstood and even made false allegations against him. Eventually, he offered his resignation as leader and this was promptly accepted. But he cheerfully accepted each of these crosses, just as he had the death of his beloved wife and the handicap of his daughter, Mary. He believed that God purifies with suffering those whom he has specially chosen.

Death

Edmund died at Mount Sion, Waterford, on 29 August 1844 and, in April 1993, Pope John Paul II declared him Venerable. Many hope that this will be a preliminary step to his being soon declared Blessed. If Edmund is some day reckoned among the Blessed it will not only be for the great works of mercy and charity he performed but, even more, because of his patient and cheerful acceptance of the sufferings God sent him. Nor must it be thought that what he achieved was accomplished because the circumstances were ideal or the odds always in his favour: no, indeed! It was, rather, because of his perseverance and heroic efforts. Indeed, it could be said that many of his good deeds and achievements were effected in spite of difficulties, misunderstandings and opposition.

A Waterford Quaker who witnessed Edmund's funeral summed up his life with remarkable insight. He wrote:

> The display of feelings manifested at the interment of Brother Rice shows that the people are neither forgetful nor ungrateful. No wonder, as they see the extraordinary change brought about mainly by his instrumentality. The Roman Catholics believe he was a messenger from God.... Mr Rice is not dead! He lives! Yes, he lives the highest, noblest and greatest life. He lives in the noble band of Christian workmen to whom he has bequeathed his spirit and his work.

NOTES ON CONTRIBUTORS

Brennock, Ruth: parent, living in Midleton, Co Cork; trained facilitator and group leader; formerly secretary of Federation of CBS Parents Councils; more recently President of National Parents' Council (Post-Primary); popular speaker on subject of PTAs and parent education; special interests include training of parents for participation in PTAs and school boards of management.

Daly, His Eminence Cahal B.: b. 1917; ordained priest 22 June 1941; ordained Bishop of Ardagh and Clonmacnois 16 July 1967; installed Bishop of Down and Connor 17 October 1982; installed Archbishop of Armagh 16 December 1990; created Cardinal 28 June 1991; author of several books and numerous articles.

Feheney, John Matthew FPM: b. 1932; Presentation Brother; Director Christian Formation Resource Centre, Cork; publications include *Ranahans of Iverus* (Cork: Iverus Publications, 1987), *Pastoral Care* (3 vols) (Dublin: Folens, 1994) and numerous articles in educational (e.g. *British Journal of Educational Studies*) and historical (e.g. *Irish Historical Studies*) journals.

Flanagan, Mary Bernadette: b. 1958; BA, MA; Presentation Sister; Associate lecturer in spirituality Milltown Institute of Theology and Philosophy; special interests include urban spirituality.

Humphreys, Tony: BA, HDipEd, MA, PhD; Consultant clinical psychologist in private practice and specialist lecturer for Health Care Professions and Teachers at University College, Cork, and Mary Immaculate College of Education, Limerick. Publications include *A Different Kind of Teacher* (1993); *Self-Esteem – the Key to your Child's Education* (1994); *The Family – Love It and Leave It* (1994).

Hyland, Aine (nee Donlon): b. 1942; BA, HDipEd, MEd, PhD; Professor of Education University College, Cork; Publications include: *Irish Educational Documents,* vols 1, 2 and 3 (with K. Milne *et al*) (Dublin: CICE, 1987); general editor *Irish Educational Studies.* She has published many articles on Irish education from a historical and policy perspective in educational journals.

Kelleher, Michael J.: BSc, MPhil, MD, FRCPsych, FRCPI; educated at Presentation College, Cork, UCC and London University; consultant psychiatrist Maudsley and Bethlem Royal Hospitals; lecturer in psychiatry University College, Cork; clinical director psychiatric services North Lee catchment area, Southern Health Board; researched widely in psychiatric medicine and published numerous articles and research papers on different aspects of psychiatry in scientific journals.

Lee, John Joseph: b. 1942, Tralee; educated Gormanston and UCD(BA), Institute for European History, Mainz, and Peterhouse, Cambridge (MA); MRIA; Professor of History and Head of History Department UCC; senator; author of numerous books and articles including, *The Modernisation of Irish Society 1848-1918* (Dublin: Gill & Macmillan, 1973, 2nd ed., 1989); *Ireland 1912-85: Politics and Society* (Cambridge: Cambridge University Press, 1989).

McClelland, Vincent Alan: MA, PhD: Professor of Educational Studies and Dean of the School of Education, University of Hull; has published widely on the history and philosophy of education, religious education and ecclesiastical history; publications include *English Roman Catholics and Higher Education, 1830-1903* (Oxford: Oxford University Press); *Cardinal Manning: His Public Life and Influence, 1865-92* (Oxford: Oxford University Press); *Christian Education in a Pluralist Society* (Routledge) etc; editor of *Recusant History* and *Aspects of Education.*

McVerry, Peter SJ: b. 1944; BSc, HDipEd; Works in Jesuit Centre for Faith and Justice, mainly on issues relating to young people; author of *We Must Decide: The Development of the Roman Catholic Teaching on Social Justice* (Dublin: Jesuit Centre for Faith and Justice, 1986); *Spike Island – the Answer to What?* (Dublin: Jesuit Centre for Faith and Justice, 1985); runs hostels for young homeless boys in Dublin.

O'Keeffe, Thomas: b. 1946; educated Marino Institute of Education (Teacher's Certificate); UCC (BA, HDipEd); teacher at Coláiste Chríost Rí, Cork; studying for MEd (Hull and CFRC).

Ryan, Liam: b. 1936, Cappamore, Co Limerick; educated St Flannan's College, Maynooth College and St Louis University; formerly lecturer in Sociology UCC; Professor of Sociology in Maynooth since 1969. Publications include *Irish Attitudes and Values* (Dublin: Dominican Publications, 1985), *Counselling the Adolescent in a Changing Ireland* (Dublin: Institute of Guidance Counsellors, 1993), and numerous articles in journals.

Steele, Frank Joseph: b. Cork, 1943; Educated Marino Institute of Education (Teacher's Certificate); UCC (BA, MA), Keble College, Oxford (D Phil); Principal St Aidan's Community College, Cork; tutor and occasional lecturer MEd Programme CFRC (Cork); Associate Presentation Brothers.